Elton John
The life and music of a legendary performer

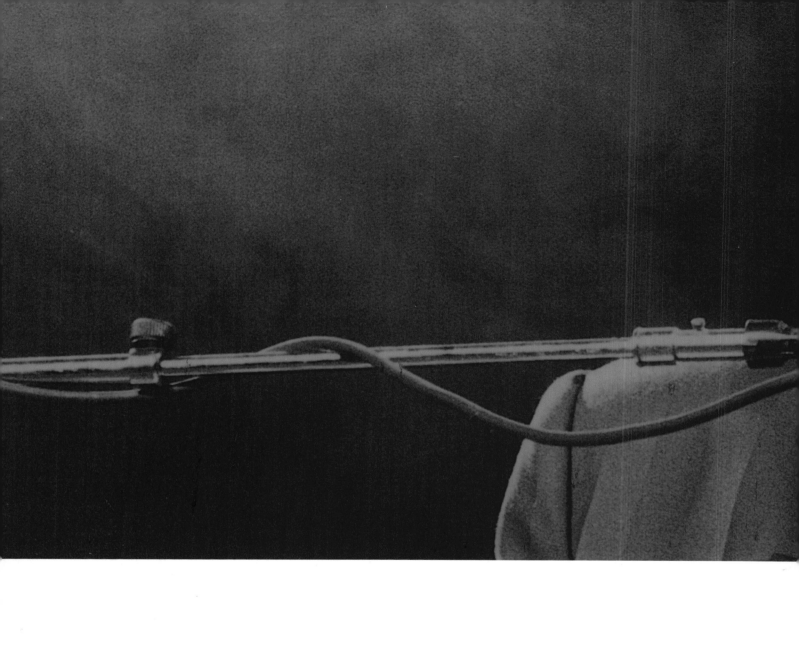

Elton John
The life and music of a legendary performer

Michael Heatley

CLB

Commissioning Editor: Jane Alexander
Production: Gerald Hughes, Karen Staff, Ruth Arthur

Produced for Quadrillion Publishing Ltd by
The Design Revolution, Brighton, England
Editor: Ian Whitelaw
Design: Lindsey Johns, Fiona Roberts
Commissioned photography: Jeremy Thomas, Brighton, England
Picture research: James Clarke

Elton John 5095

Published in 1998 by CLB International
Copyright © 1998 CLB International
A division of Quadrillion Publishing Ltd., Godalming Business
Centre, Woolsack Way, Godalming, Surrey, England, GU7 1XW

This edition distributed in the USA by Quadrillion Publishing Inc.,
230 Fifth Avenue, New York, NY 10001

contents

★ Overture

When Britain lost its inspirational Princess of Wales in August 1997, the forest of flowers outside the Royal palaces silently articulated the nation's grief. Only one man could put it into words and music, even though the words were those of his long-time lyricist—and that was Elton John.

The record-breaking success of 'Candle In The Wind 97', now the biggest-selling single of all time, proves what fans knew already—that no-one sums up the popular mood better. Ironically, Elton's career in music started the same year Princess Diana was born (1961). Since then he's risen from backing musician, through jobbing songwriter, to showbiz legend. More than that, he's a legend with a heart of gold, whose singles royalties have long gone to fund research against AIDS.

His private and public *personae* may often have been poles apart, but Elton has consistently evoked the age-old variety slogan "the show must go on", battling against adversity to present his inimitable public face to an adoring world. Problems with drink, drugs, and bulimia have been faced and overcome, while the threat of throat cancer in 1986 paradoxically spurred him to a colossal live vocal performance in front of a 10 million live TV audience. Perhaps most crucially of all, he's overcome trial by tabloid to vindicate his reputation after his name was blackened by false sex slurs.

There's an irony in the personal connection his public have always made with his message, from first hit 'Your Song' to the Diana tribute, for the words he sings are someone else's: his enduring relationship with lyricist Bernie Taupin is one relative constant in his ever-changing world. This book, published as Elton John receives a well-earned knighthood for his musical and charitable achievements, looks at the music and the master showman behind it.

Left: The public showmanship and private complexity of Elton John are highlighted in this picture, juxtaposing the 'off-duty' Elton with some of his most famous stage gear.

Above: In character and in full voice, Elton the entertainer gives his all—as he has done in a solo career spanning three eventful decades.

It was a curious business, growing up in post-war

Britain. After almost seven years of conflict, the adult population could now at last bring children into a world at peace—even if relations with Russia were fast freezing over. But with rationing still a fact of life for some years to come, and with all young men between 18 and 21 obliged to do at least 18 months' national service, memories of the war years were hard to shake off.

The military still played a large role in the life of the Dwight family. Stanley Dwight was a Flight Lieutenant in the Royal Air Force, and so was frequently away from home serving King and country. In January 1945, with the end of hostilities in sight, he had married Sheila Harris, and they had made their first home with her parents in Pinner Hill Road, where a son, Reginald Kenneth, came into the world on 25 March 1947.

His mother and grandmother encouraged the only child to amuse himself as they went about their daily business, and with the family piano close at hand, early promise was soon evident. By the age of four, the young Reginald was proudly playing his party piece, the 'Skater's Waltz', for visitors. After spending a couple of years on an RAF base, at Lyneham in Wiltshire, the Dwights set up home on their own in Northwood Hills, near Pinner, but the marriage could not survive Stanley's frequent absences.

No Man About the House

In the light of his later lifestyle, much has since been made of the female-dominated environment in which the future Elton John grew up. Indeed there have been instances during his career when he has publicly railed against his father for not being around during his formative years. (Stanley later remarried and had a second family, with whom he was very happy). Nonetheless, there was to be

some kind of reconciliation between them before Stanley's death in the early 1990s, based on their common love of football.

At 50, appreciating the problems of his parents' relationship more keenly than before, Elton looked back fondly and "wished we could have said more". He could see that there were "two sides to every story", but as a youngster he associated his father's presence with marital disharmony and at the time he automatically took his mother's side.

If the young Reg Dwight wanted an alternative role model, there was a national figure in the family in the shape of an older cousin—and a footballer, at that! Roy played professional football for Fulham, and the Dwights were a close enough clan for a wedding picture (with six year-old Reg acting as pageboy) to be one of the oldest commercially available photographs from his childhood. Roy achieved fame in a brief and terrible way when he scored in the 1959 FA Cup Final while playing for Nottingham Forest against Luton Town and suffered a broken leg. Ten-man Forest (this was before the age of substitutes) held on to record a 2-1 victory, going one better than Watford,

"I lost touch with my father. There was a wide rift between us."

who fell at the final hurdle 25 years on when Elton was chairman. Yet his abiding love of the game clearly dates from this early hero-worship.

Dreams of following in his cousin's sporting footsteps were beyond the reach of the stocky youngster, so he sought another way out of the suburban rut. As with so many other teenagers, music would prove his passport to freedom. But while many a future pop star was picking up an acoustic guitar and scrubbing along with skiffle king Lonnie Donegan, Reg's chosen instrument was—what else?—the piano.

While the days found him studying at Pinner County Grammar, a 1958 scholarship to the Royal Academy of Music meant his Saturdays would be football-less for the foreseeable future. He was already aware of the possibilities outside classical music—indeed, he was to confess on television, in 1997's *An Audience With Elton John*, recorded in front of a host of guest celebrities, that his fingers were always too stubby to pursue a career in 'straight' music—and he cut his solo performing teeth playing Jim Reeves numbers to unheeding drinkers at the Northwood Hills Hotel in Pinner. It was an invaluable training ground, if somewhat repetitive, and when he came to audition for Liberty Records in 1967 he resorted to the Reeves songbook, as he could guarantee to remember the words under pressure!

Above The house at 55 Pinner Hill Road that Reg Dwight called home for the first years of his life and where he first encountered the piano. It was actually the home of grand-parents Fred and Ivy Harris, but the Dwights were to move to Northwood Hills before their marriage foundered.

Left The Northwood Hills Hotel, where the young school-age Reg played ballads of the Jim Reeves/Ray Charles variety on Fridays, Saturdays, and Sundays. The funds raised enabled him to buy his first electric piano. He happily took requests, learning at an early age how to build up a rapport with his audience.

Right Winifred Atwell, an unlikely early inspiration for Reg Dwight in an era when the guitar already ruled supreme. Her instrumental, 'Poor People Of Paris', was the first piece of music he'd take pride in learning to play from scratch. She emigrated to Australia, where they'd later meet.

Below The influence of Little Richard, the Georgia Peach, is clear from the piano-straddling moment captured here. Elton described dueting with Richard on 'The Power', a John-Taupin song written for the 1993 album 'Duets', as "one of the highlights of my career."

Early Idols

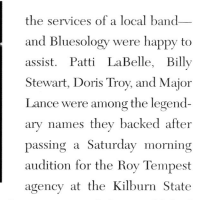

Influential figures in the pre-rock era had come from his mother's record collection—the likes of Winifred Atwell, Frankie Laine and Rosemary Clooney. But when she brought home records by Bill Haley and Elvis Presley, the wide-eyed youngster's delight knew no bounds. His own first purchases were Jackie Wilson's 'Reet Petite' and Danny and the Juniors' 'At The Hop', while the later arrival of rock'n'roll pianists Jerry Lee Lewis and Little Richard confirmed that sitting behind a piano was no obstacle to stardom—even if the youngster was, as yet, still forbidden to put his foot on top of it!

Seeking further musical satisfaction, and with pop clearly on an upward curve, he formed a local group—the Corvettes—with guitarist/vocalist Stuart Brown. Though Brown would go on to front a band called Cochise in the 1970s, this particular aggregation (named after a then-popular brand of shaving cream!) wouldn't make it beyond the neighborhood youth-club and coffee-bar circuit, the landlord of the Northwood Hills Hotel remaining immune to numerous requests for engagements.

The step up to semi-professional status came in 1961 with Bluesology, a group named after a Django Reinhardt jazz standard. Stuart Brown was there again, with Rex Bishop (bass) and Mick Inkpen (drums) initially making up the numbers. With most of the key musical moves being made on the other side of the Atlantic, a constant stream of soul stars were touring Britain, invariably needing the services of a local band—and Bluesology were happy to assist. Patti LaBelle, Billy Stewart, Doris Troy, and Major Lance were among the legendary names they backed after passing a Saturday morning audition for the Roy Tempest agency at the Kilburn State Cinema, and it was a period that would find later musical echoes in the likes of 'Philadelphia Freedom' and 'Sleeping With The Past'.

While making a living playing four gruelling shows a night, Bluesology were not without ambitions of their own. They cut their first single, 'Come Back Baby', in 1965, its release by Fontana in July being the first time the name of Reg Dwight appeared on a record label. It would later be exhumed for the 1990 box set, 'To Be Continued…', and it is said by its writer to demonstrate exactly why he needed the services of a lyricist! But despite two further releases (most notably February 1966's 'Mr Frantic') Bluesology remained firmly a backing outfit.

At the end of 1966 they linked with a star from rather nearer home than their usual clientele—London-based Long John Baldry. He rejigged the band dramatically, bringing in guitarists Neil Hubbard and Caleb Quaye, drummer Pete Gavin and horn players Elton Dean and Marc Charig, but when the Humperdinck-esque big ballad 'Let The Heartaches Begin' reached Number 1 in late 1967 Elton could see the writing on the wall. With Baldry intent on taking the cabaret route, he needed a more satisfactory outlet for his talents—and he found it when, on auditioning for Liberty Records as a songwriter, he was put in touch with lyricist Bernie Taupin.

"As Baldry's style changed towards the soft ballady stuff, we moved into cabaret and it was really beginning to bring me down."

Above The tour program from the UK tour on which Bluesology, Reg Dwight's first serious group backed Little Richard on a UK tour. The text above their photo reads: "Bluesology, a group of six young talented musicians, take their name from the title of a record by the famous French jazz guitarist Django Reinhardt. 'We play blues music mainly after the style of Jimmy Witherspoon, Memphis Slim and Muddy Waters with, dare we say it, a slight jazz flavour', they explain."

Left Doris Troy was another of the soul artists Bluesology would back on the grueling UK gig circuit. Stateside stars would often be booked to play double-headers in two different (though neighboring) venues, giving them up to four sets per evening to fulfill. It was a grounding that would serve him well, and his love of black music resurfaced regularly, most notably in 1989's 'Sleeping With The Past'.

Right Scots songstress Lulu in Eurovision mode. Though the John-Taupin composition 'I Can't Go On Living Without You' lost out to the ultimately victorious and genre-defining 'Boom-Bang-A-Bang', Lulu never forgot, and she was set to be relaunched on the Rocket label in 1998 with a specially composed song.

Below Patti LaBelle (center) enjoyed two careers, first with the BlueBelles and then in the 1970s with an eponymous glam-funk trio. She'd repay the backing she got from Bluesology on UK tours by guesting on 1975's 'Rock Of The Westies'.

Right The Inkspots were another American act to enjoy backing from Bluesology on British tours. The Roy Tempest Agency set up the tours, and it was a thrill for Reg and his bandmates to play with such legendary names, even though the pay was less than generous.

Left Long John Baldry, the British blues singer who adopted Bluesology as his backing band. His maudlin 1967 chart-topper 'Let The Heartaches Begin' was emphatically not the kind of music Elton wanted to play, though they remained friends and Elton later produced a post-hit album for him.

Left The earliest known publicity picture of Elton John and his lyricist Bernie Taupin together. They met in the reception of Dick James Studios, went round the corner to a café called the Lancaster Grill and "just talked." It would be another year before Bernie moved down to London, leaving theirs a 'songwriting by mail' relationship for the time being.

Below King Crimson, the progressive rock group founded by guitarist Robert Fripp (second from left). Elton was so unsure of his future as a solo pop star that in early 1970 he auditioned for the group, but was beaten to the vocalist's position by Greg Lake (pictured third from right).

"I was impressed by Bernie's work.
And I was keen to team up with him."

Above When Bernie Taupin came down from Lincolnshire to make a go of professional songwriting, he lodged with Elton, his mother, and stepfather in 30a Frome Court, Northwood Hills, apart from a spell in an Islington flat with Elton and his fiancee Linda Woodrow. The story of that relationship and its end was told in 'Someone Saved My Life Tonight'.

Opposite The pair attempt to smolder in another publicity shot. It was an era when non-playing lyricists were employed by a number of top bands, including Cream (Pete Brown) and Procol Harum (Keith Reid). Taupin would later try his hand at music, forming a band called Farm Dogs in the mid 1990s.

Lincolnshire-bred Bernie had nearly failed to answer the Liberty ad in New Musical Express: legend has it that his mother fished his letter out of the wastepaper bin! Though three years younger than Reg, he'd lived a more adventurous life, having left school early and been through jobs ranging from chicken farm hand to working for a newspaper as a print operator. "My dad was a farmer," he later said, "but I guess I had bigger plans." His inspiration to turn poetry into song lyrics came from Radio Luxembourg, then the trendiest radio station around.

Fascinatingly, the first two dozen Dwight-Taupin compositions came together by post, the pair not meeting face to face until months later. The results have never been heard officially—titles like 'Regimental Sergeant Zippo', 'The Witch's House', and 'Mr Lightning Strikerman'

may explain why—but they were promising enough for the pair to be employed as staff writers for Dick James Music at his London office. The delighted duo failed to take independent legal advice when signing the contract—they were being paid for what they enjoyed, after all—and this was to be something they would bitterly regret in years to come.

That being said, Dick James had been the Beatles' music publisher with Northern Songs and so had a great track record for anyone wanting to get their work heard. Indeed, Lulu would perform one of the duo's songs, 'I Can't Go On Living Without You', on 1969's Song For Europe—and though 'Boom Bang-A-Bang' was the number that went forward to win Eurovision, Cilla Black thought the offering good enough to record. Other artists, including actor Edward Woodward, followed her lead with other songs, while Reg took a couple of shots at the chart in his own right: March 1968's 'I've Been Loving You' and January 1969's 'Lady Samantha' were both released by Philips, but neither caught the public imagination.

Goodbye Reg, Hello Elton

Nonetheless, people in the business were sitting up and taking notice. US act Three Dog Night covered 'Lady Samantha' with some success, backing its writer's admission that it was "the first song I'd been involved with that I was really pleased with". The singles were also his first as Elton John, having borrowed components of the names of Elton Dean and Long John Baldry to create an identity with which he was more comfortable.

Bernie had by now moved south and, having initially lodged at Elton's parents' house, was now sharing an Islington, north London, flat with his writing partner—and a third person!

Right Elton and Bernie pose with Dick James (right) and his son Stephen (left). The DJM organization's role as managers, music publishers, and record label put all the duo's eggs in one basket, and a court action in the mid 1980s would seek to redress what Elton and Bernie saw as injustices in the contracts they were happy to sign when unknown.

Below Elton John faces the music as he celebrates the release of 'Tumbleweed Connection', his second album of 1970 and the third in 15 months. A punishing work schedule would see this two-album-a-year output continue unabated until the mid 1970s, seemingly without any diminishing returns on the creativity front.

Left The Elton John Band, namely drummer Nigel Olsson and bassist Dee Murray (standing) who would make it on to a studio record for the first time on 'Tumbleweed Connection' and remain the core of his band until the mid 1970s. Olsson had played with popsters Plastic Penny and rockers Uriah Heep, Murray with the unknown Mirage. The pair first met when playing with the Spencer Davis Group.

Center Dusty Springfield, a 1960s icon whose picture used to adorn Reg Dwight's bedroom wall, was co-opted to sing backing vocals on 'Tumbleweed Connection' alongside Madeline Bell (Blue Mink), ace session-man Tony Burrows, and Lesley Duncan.

Left Elton takes Little Richard's piano posing to extremes during a high-profile gig at London's Edmonton Sundown in 1971. His delicate studio creations were already at odds with a stage persona that could only be described as extrovert. A March Festival Hall appearance, his first with string accompaniment, had been somewhat more sedate, however.

Linda Woodrow was a statuesque blonde whom today's tabloids might label a pickled-onion heiress (her family owned Epicure Pickles). The pair had met at a Bluesology gig in Sheffield, and had been scheduled to marry. But Elton could not go through with it: his attempted gas-oven suicide (later chronicled in 'Someone Saved My Life Tonight') was a cry for help. It was heeded by his mother, who sent stepfather Fred Farebrother—dubbed 'Derf' by Elton in happier times—to remove him, Bernie and their possessions and bring them back to temporary refuge with them.

If his private life was already becoming more complicated, the year of 1969 found Elton up to his neck in work. He was in great demand to play and sing on budget-price albums offering soundalike covers of current hits (a selection would be issued in 1994 as 'Reg Dwight's Piano Goes Pop'). On a completely different musical tack, he auditioned for progressive group King Crimson, and in the meantime played session piano for Tom Jones and for the Hollies. One of the latter's songs, 'He Ain't Heavy He's My Brother', would be a delayed chart-topper nearly 20 years later thanks to a Miller lager commercial—but the idea of a Number 1 single in his own right was still a long way away.

Despite these diversions, the sessions for his first album, 'Empty Sky', were foremost in

Below Manchester's Hollies played a large part in the early career of Elton John. Having joined DJM via connections with the group's Gralto publishing company (named after Graham Nash, Allan Clarke, and Tony Hicks, the front line pictured left to right below), he then played session piano on a number of their hits after Nash had quit to seek Stateside fame.

Left A still from the 1971 film *Friends*, which gave Elton John his first soundtrack experience. Elton described the film, a tale of teenagers in love, directed by Lewis Gilbert, as "a cute little film." The album reached Number 36 in the States, but the fact that this was the fourth Elton John LP in just over a year gave rise to accusations of overkill.

Elton's mind. Although the album, released in June 1969, failed to break any sales records (apparently only 4,000 were sold), it was a foot on the ladder. And no time was lost in coming up with a follow-up. Released in April 1970, 'Elton John' was the album that really launched the success story, combining Elton and Bernie with another creative duo in producer Gus Dudgeon and arranger Paul Buckmaster. Both had been involved in David Bowie's chart-topping 'Space Oddity' single, and the album they helped to create showcased the singer-songwriter's style perfectly. With Carole King and James Taylor setting the pace Stateside, it was a good time to be singing your own songs.

The standout tracks on 'Elton John' were 'Border Song', the first single and a gospelly number soon to be covered by Aretha Franklin,

the Leon Russell-influenced 'Take Me To The Pilot', and the second single, 'Your Song'. Legend has it that Bernie Taupin wrote this at the breakfast table, but whatever the truth it gave him a Number 8 US hit (Number 7 at home), while its inclusion took the parent album past 250,000 sales—a real improvement on its predecessor.

Next, though, came a couple of diversions from the main theme. Film producer Lewis Gilbert, impressed by 'Elton John', asked the team to contribute to his new movie *Friends*. Though Taupin saw neither script nor film, a number of songs made it on to the album, with Buckmaster plucking out snatches of linking melody to pad things out. Then came '17-11-70', a live radio broadcast for a New York station that turned out so well it was released to the public the following year.

"'Elton John' was the album that really launched the success story, combining Elton and Bernie with another creative duo ..."

Elton John

Musicians Elton John (piano, harpsichord, vocals), Terry Cox (drums), Barry Morgan (drums), Dave Richmond (bass), Frank Clark (acoustic guitar and bass), Colin Green (guitar and Spanish guitar), Clive Hicks (12-string, acoustic, and rhythm guitar), Roland Harker (guitar), Skaila Kanga (harp), Alan Weichill (bass), Caleb Quaye (lead guitar), Alan Parker (rhythm guitar), Dennis Lopez (percussion), Diana Lewis (Moog synthesizer), Brian Dee (organ), Paul Buckmaster (cello), Tex Navarra (percussion), Les Hurdle (bass), Barbara Moore Choir (vocals), Madeline Bell, Lesley Duncan, Kay Garner, Tony Burrows, Tony Hazzard and Roger Cook (all backing vocals) • **Recorded at** Trident Studios, Soho • **Top 20 hit singles** 'Your Song' (US 8, UK 7) • **Unusual fact** 'Grey Seal', recorded during the January album sessions but omitted from the final track selection, would be re-recorded and released on 'Goodbye Yellow Brick Road' • **Track listing** Your Song • I Need You To Turn To • Take Me To The Pilot • No Shoestrings On Louise • First Episode At Hienton • Sixty Years On • Border Song • The Greatest Discovery • The Cage • The King Must Die • **Commentary** The staggering number of session players employed to record 'Elton John' did not detract from its quality—especially surprising given that the whole album was recorded live. Much was down to the organizational abilities of producer Gus Dudgeon, for whom this was a first project with Elton. Their relationship was to continue through nine more studio and two live albums, and he became a director of Elton's Rocket Records • While 'Empty Sky' had been a UK-only release, this album was issued by MCA in the States on their Uni label, charting there before it hit at home. The album was recorded in just 55 hours at a reported cost of some £6,500, and it remains in print to this day—not the most successful Elton John album ever, but arguably the most significant • **Elsewhere in 1970...** Jimi Hendrix and Janis Joplin are big name rock fatalities • Diana Ross leaves the Supremes • The Who record a University gig for their 'Live At Leeds' album • The Beatles' final new single, 'Let It Be', is released • Simon and Garfunkel release 'Bridge Over Troubled Water'

Released April 1970

Chart Position UK 11

Chart Position US 4

Producer Gus Dudgeon

It was already becoming obvious that, once on stage, the mild-mannered, bespectacled boy from Pinner was potentially a master showman. A week-long August residency at Los Angeles' fabled Troubadour club (capacity 250 at most) had drawn more stars than the average constellation, with Leon Russell, Gordon Lightfoot, Quincy Jones, and the Beach Boys paying tribute to the newcomer. Critics concurred, and the buzz started spreading: from now on Elton would be bigger in the States than in his native lands. The other interesting thing to come out of the week was Bernie meeting his future wife, Maxine Feibelman.

Live albums and film soundtracks notwithstanding, the real follow-ups to 'Elton John' were 'Tumbleweed Connection' (February 1971) and 'Madman Across The Water' (October 1971). The former had something of a concept feel, and rock critic John Tobler has suggested it may well have inspired the Eagles to create 'Desperado', another album with a Wild West theme, a matter of two years later.

'Tumbleweed' highlights included a cover version of 'Love Song', performed as a duet with its writer, Lesley Duncan, while the self-penned 'Country Comfort' would itself be covered by close friend Rod Stewart on his 'Gasoline Alley' album. 'Burn Down The Mission', meanwhile, would become a live favorite, often incorporating verses of the Beatles' 'Get Back' and Elvis's 'My Baby Left Me' to crowd-pleasing effect. It was already clear that the stage and studio versions of Elton John were worlds apart.

'Madman' spawned two US hit singles in 'Levon' and 'Tiny Dancer', the latter written by Bernie about Maxine, which reached Numbers 24 and 41 respectively. Other outstanding tracks included 'Holiday Inn'—a paean to the temporary home of many a rock musician—and the album title track, the meaning of which Elton would cheerfully admit had passed him by. "He just gives me the lyric, we never bother to discuss it" was his assessment of the burgeoning John-Taupin writing partnership.

Successful Line-up

With Elton contractually obliged to turn in two albums a year, it is amazing that the standard of his releases remained so uniformly high—and, aside from Taupin's lyrics, part of the reason was the tight-knit rhythm section of Dee Murray (bass, real name David Murray Oates) and Nigel Olsson (drums). Olsson's varied CV included stints with Plastic Penny and heavy-metal giants Uriah Heep, but the pair had worked together in the (post-Steve Winwood) Spencer Davis Group and they were clearly a more than compatible team.

A trio of piano, bass, and drums is a regular sight on the jazz circuit, but it put an awful lot of the performing load on Elton's shoulders in the effort to create a rock spectacle. A guitarist was the obvious addition to make, and Elton thought big by inviting Jeff Beck to rehearse with them, but the ex-Yardbird elected not to join the happy throng. (It has been said that he wanted to replace Nigel with Cozy Powell,

Left Jeff Beck, the mercurial guitarist who came to fame with the Yardbirds and then his own band with Rod Stewart, was briefly up for being the Elton John Band's six-stringer, but the liaison lasted just one rehearsal. Davey Johnstone would get the gig, while Elton and Jeff would bump into each other through the years, most recently appearing on Jon Bon Jovi's 1990 album 'Blaze Of Glory'.

Opposite A dungareed Elton plays the Revolution Club at the time of his eponymous second album. His dress sense would develop through the 1970s to produce the showman we know today.

Left By January 1971 Elton John was front-page news. This copy of *Disc and Music Echo*, then one of the leading weekly music papers, lauded him as "the man who made the most impact in pop during 1970". There was, of course, much more to come—kicking off with no fewer than three albums (one live, one film, one studio) in 1971.

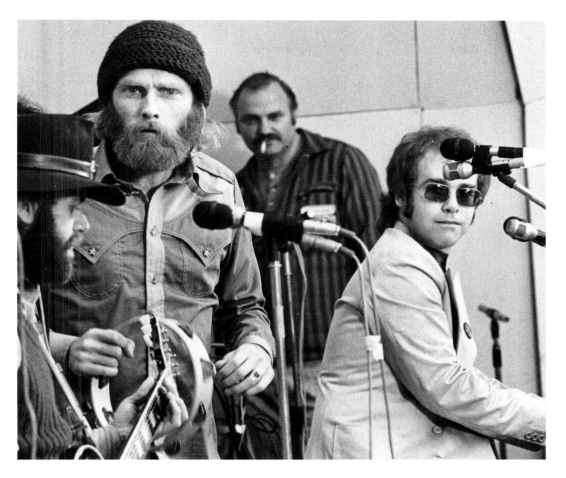

> "A live highlight came when he was invited to support the Beach Boys..."

and a loyal Elton was having none of it.) Another high-profile possibility might have been Marc Bolan, but the T Rex leader was doing very nicely thank you. Even so, Elton was happy to lend a hand—or, more accurately, two—when the 'boppin' Elf' was booked for a *Top Of The Pops* Christmas appearance at the end of 1971 to promote the chart-topping 'Get It On'.

New Friends and Old

A live highlight came when he was invited to support the Beach Boys in an outdoor concert at Crystal Palace Stadium, south London. The group, whose harmonies were influential on so much of Elton's music (and who would indeed contribute to 'Don't Let The Sun Go Down On

Me') gladly allowed their protégé to guest on stage with them, to the delight of a large crowd. While Elton was hobnobbing with long-standing hitmakers, his old boss (and part namesake) Long John Baldry was down on his luck, and he persuaded Elton and Rod Stewart, another former colleague, to help him out by performing on and producing a side apiece of a new album. The appropriately titled 'It Ain't Easy' wouldn't pull up any trees sales-wise, but the reversal of fortunes proved not only that Elton had been right to leave the security of Bluesology to strike out on his own but also, to paraphrase the stockbrokers' warning, that pop fortunes can go down as well as up. The Rocket Man was soon to find he'd not yet reached his peak...

1972 was a year of change.

The month of May saw the official demise of Reginald Kenneth Dwight as, by deed poll, he officially became Elton Hercules John. A mansion in Wokingham, Berkshire, was also christened Hercules, a name that he had picked at random as "an alternative… some people might not like to call me Elton." The drive at Hercules was filled with famous names—Rolls, Daimler, Bentley, Mercedes—but he was seldom around to drive them. In his absence, mum and stepfather Fred moved in, the latter wielding the occasional paintbrush as necessary.

Previous page Elton and Bernie revel in the success of their first chart-topping album, 1973's 'Don't Shoot Me I'm Only The Piano Player'. All told, it was their eighth release in three and a half years, a series of albums that had established Elton as an international act.

Right The band, including new guitarist Davey Johnstone (right, back row) and guest 'Legs' Larry Smith (in hat) relax before the 1972 Royal Variety show at the London Palladium. Former Bonzo Dog Doo-Dah Band member Smith reproduced his studio tap-dance on 'I Think I'm Gonna Kill Myself'.

Below These boots were made for talkin'! DJ Noel Edmonds welcomes Elton to his Kings Road, London record shop for a 1973 album signing session. US officials had shown an interest in the pianist's stack heels when he flew in the previous year, searching them for drugs!

As Elton's notoriety increased, especially in the States, so his public persona blossomed. Far from the shy, introverted, bespectacled pianist of old, he was now taking every opportunity to dress in glitter and lamé, leap about behind his piano (no stool required) and generally behave, as Bob Dylan might have put it, like a Rolling Stone. This extrovert side wasn't something that had yet been fully reflected in his recorded output, but his group's musical muscle was significantly reinforced in February 1972 when they finally recruited a guitarist to the line-up.

Blond 20-year-old Scot Davey Johnstone had previous 'form' with folk group Magna Carta, who had pressed him into service with a variety of stringed instruments, including banjo, sitar, mandolin, and even the medieval lute. While such virtuosity and versatility were to come in handy, it was as a rock guitarist that Elton primarily cast him—and, having 'auditioned' successfully on 'Madman', where he shared the billing with several others, he joined the band full-time for their next appointment in the recording studio.

The chosen venue for the recording was the Chateau d'Herouville, 30 miles from Paris, which proved so conducive to creativity that the nickname Elton gave it, the 'Honky Chateau', eventually became the album's title. The recording was done and dusted in just three weeks, with impressive results.

Walking Tall in the USA

Elton had never been an imposing figure, but glam-rock's penchant for platform shoes helped him add inches where it counted—at ground level! Yet even he might have thought he'd gone a little too far when, on arrival at Los Angeles International airport for the next bout of US touring, police searched his eight-inch heels for possible hidden drugs! Having weathered that storm with admirable grace, he stopped off at Houston to take lunch with Apollo 15 pilot Al Warden and inspect the forthcoming space shot.

The reason for this new-found interest in the space programme was 'Rocket Man'—a song whose lyrics were, Bernie confessed, inspired

Above The three-man line-up of Elton, Dee, and Nigel had placed a lot of responsibility on its leaders' shoulders, both musically and in terms of visual showmanship. Their ranks would soon be swelled by Scot Davey Johnstone, and he would remain a permanent member of Elton's musical plans even after the rhythm section was brusquely dispensed with after 1975's 'Captain Fantastic'.

'I Think I'm Gonna Kill Myself' (featuring tap dancing from ex-Bonzo Dog Doo-Dah Band's 'Legs' Larry Smith) bucked the trend. French violinist Jean-Luc Ponty augmented the quartet on 'Mellow' and 'Amy', while a locally-recruited four-man horn section was also in evidence. The closing track, 'Hercules', cemented his new-found persona.

Feeling the Strain

But Hercules wasn't bearing up as well as his mythical namesake to the two albums a year and constant touring schedule. He'd been fighting glandular fever as he recorded 'Honky Chateau', wanting to "get it over with", and admits that when he arrived in Malibu in June for a well-earned break he was "on the verge of a crack-up". He soon regained his characteristic zest for life, though, and among the visitors to his rented mansion were childhood hero Groucho Marx and David Cassidy, the teen idol *du jour*, who could share his experiences of fame and its pressures.

Back in Britain, he found time to make a cameo appearance in Marc Bolan's film *Born To Boogie*, directed by Ringo Starr, before returning yet again to the Chateau to record. Groucho Marx had inspired the title of the new album before it was even recorded—and homage was duly paid when on the cover, underneath the cinema portico advertising 'Don't Shoot Me I'm Only The Piano Player', appeared a poster for the Marx Brothers' own *Go West*. The album itself saw Davey Johnstone really getting to grips with his role, allowed time and space to impress in a rock context on tracks like 'Have Mercy On The Criminal' and 'Blues For My Baby And Me'. But the spotlight, as ever, was on the singles—and what singles they were!

by little-known US writer Tom Rapp, who fronted a band called Pearls Before Swine and had written a somewhat less commercial but similarly titled effort. Taupin simply made it "a bit more a product of its time". It was this song that would build on the success of 'Your Song' and turn Elton John into a Stateside superstar, sending 'Honky Chateau' to the top of the Billboard listings—the first of three Chateau-recorded albums to attain that position.

Most of the songs found him in reflective mood, though the up-tempo 'Honky Cat' (the next single after 'Rocket Man') and jaunty, jokey

'Crocodile Rock' evoked the American teen hits of the pre-British Invasion period, with its falsetto vocal reminiscent of Pat Boone's 'Speedy Gonzales' as well as lyrical echoes of the Everly Brothers' 'Wake Up Little Suzie' and any number of Neil Sedaka classics. It was a song that, while derivative, highlighted the extrovert side of Elton, and one that struck a chord with the American public, who rewarded him with his first Number 1 single. The second, 'Daniel', traced a direct musical line of descent through 'Rocket Man' to 'Your Song'. And while 'My Love' (Paul McCartney and Wings) kept it off the top in the States, it became Elton's second highest charting UK single at Number 4. Although Bernie had been inspired by Newsweek reports of Vietnam veterans, the meaning was far from clear—not helped, perhaps, by the fact that a final verse had been chopped off the lengthy lyric!

By Royal Appointment

When the invitation for the Royal Variety Performance hit the doormat at Hercules, it was clear that Elton John was now an all-round entertainer. His appearance there in October 1972 saw him share the limelight with another of that ilk—Liberace, one of the only piano-players to hold a candle (or candelabra!) to him in terms of glitz and glitter. But early 1973 was to see Elton reveal a hitherto unsuspected facet of his personality—that of record company chief.

While he failed to don pinstripes, the launch of his own Rocket Records label was un-doubtedly serious, with manager John Reid and producer Gus Dudgeon among the shareholders. Marc Bolan, the Moody Blues, and the Rolling Stones were among the current acts to have their own labels and, though Elton

"While he failed to don pinstripes, the launch of his own Rocket Records label was undoubtedly serious."

was still contracted to DJM for the foreseeable future, he was keen to get in on the act. Unlike the typically over-the-top launch party in May at Moreton-in-Marsh railway station, signings were relatively low-key—Sheffield chanteuse Kiki Dee, Sunderland folk group Longdancer (including future Eurythmic Dave Stewart and Kai Olsson, brother of Nigel), and young Welsh singer Maldwyn Pope.

For the main man, though, the high-profile life continued apace. The year was to see even more globetrotting, and not all of it purely for touring commitments. To cut the next

Above Davey Johnstone (right) is pictured shortly after joining the ranks. His arrival apparently took Murray and Olsson by surprise, Elton introducing him as a band member while they were in France at the 'Honky Chateau'. But the newcomer's versatility and ear for melody quickly overcame any possible hostility—even if the concert money now had to be shared four ways!

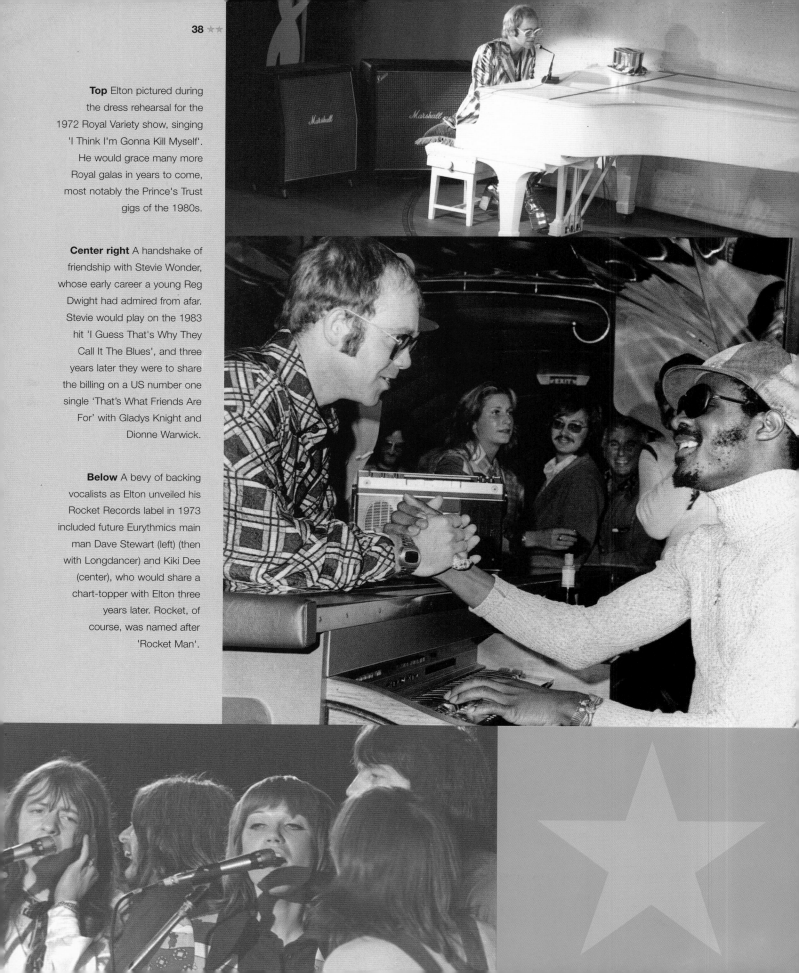

Top Elton pictured during the dress rehearsal for the 1972 Royal Variety show, singing 'I Think I'm Gonna Kill Myself'. He would grace many more Royal galas in years to come, most notably the Prince's Trust gigs of the 1980s.

Center right A handshake of friendship with Stevie Wonder, whose early career a young Reg Dwight had admired from afar. Stevie would play on the 1983 hit 'I Guess That's Why They Call It The Blues', and three years later they were to share the billing on a US number one single 'That's What Friends Are For' with Gladys Knight and Dionne Warwick.

Below A bevy of backing vocalists as Elton unveiled his Rocket Records label in 1973 included future Eurythmics main man Dave Stewart (left) (then with Longdancer) and Kiki Dee (center), who would share a chart-topper with Elton three years later. Rocket, of course, was named after 'Rocket Man'.

Left Elton, Marc Bolan, and Ringo Star toast the success of the T Rex leader's film *Born To Boogie*. Although hardly a big-screen landmark, the film saw Elton and director Starr become friends, and a John-Taupin song, 'Snookeroo', would be his gift to the amiable ex-Beatle. Elton's future film work would encompass the Grammy-winning *Lion King*—but, that being a cartoon, he was still not to appear on screen.

Left Elton shows record-company bosses don't have to wear suits as he celebrates the Rocket Records launch in the company of his band, artists, and manager John Reid. A chartered train (the symbol of the new label) had taken performers and journalists to Moreton-in-Marsh. The label would ultimately end up a vehicle for Elton alone, though it would be re-launched in the late 1990s.

Left Yet more awards and plaudits for one of the 1970s' most prolific musicians. Only 1972 and 1977 would see less than two albums unleashed on a waiting world during the decade that saw the former Reg Dwight shoot to the very top of pop.

Goodbye Yellow Brick Road

Musicians Elton John (piano, vocals), Davey Johnstone (guitar, vocals), Dee Murray (bass, vocals), Nigel Olsson (drums, vocals), David Hentschel (synthesizer), Del Newman (orchestral arrangements), Ray Cooper (tambourine), Kiki Dee (backing vocals), Leroy Gomez (saxophone) • **Recorded at** Strawberry Studios, France (aka the Chateau) • **Top 20 hit singles** 'Saturday Night's Alright For Fighting' (UK 7, US 12), 'Bennie And The Jets' (US 1), 'Candle In The Wind' (UK 11), 'Goodbye Yellow Brick Road' (UK 6, US 2) • **Unusual fact** 'Bennie And The Jets' was initially a US-only release, prompted by a Detroit DJ who claimed it got a big response from black audiences • **Track listing** Funeral For A Friend • Love Lies Bleeding • Candle In The Wind • Bennie And The Jets • Goodbye Yellow Brick Road • This Song Has No Title • Grey Seal • Jamaica Jerk-Off • I've Seen That Movie Too • Sweet Painted Lady • The Ballad Of Danny Bailey • Dirty Little Girl • All The Girls Love Alice • Your Sister Can't Twist (But She Can Rock'n'Roll) • Saturday Night's Alright For Fighting • Roy Rogers • Social Disease • Harmony • **Commentary** In the States, where it was Elton's third Number 1 album, 'Goodbye Yellow Brick Road' knocked the Rolling Stones' 'Goat's Head Soup' off the top. In Britain, it was TV teen idol David Cassidy that gave way. Either way, no-one else was going to have much of a look-in before Christmas while this song-stuffed double album held sway. It had been planned to be recorded in Jamaica, where the Rolling Stones had cut their album, but technical problems caused a rethink and an Atlantic crossing • The lead single 'Saturday Night's Alright For Fighting' was cut with Elton standing at the microphone to encourage his musicians to rock out: piano was added later. Even the Who's cover version for the 'Two Rooms' tribute album can't measure up • **Elsewhere in 1973...** 'New Dylan' Bruce Springsteen's first album was released in the UK • Eric Clapton returned after drug addiction • The Everly Brothers split up after 16 chart years • Unknown Queen released their first single • Slade cornered the seasonal market with the first release of 'Merry Xmas Everybody' • CBGB's, New York's legendary punk club, opened for business.

Released October 1973

Chart Position UK 1 (2 weeks)

Chart Position US 1 (8 weeks)

Producer Gus Dudgeon

album, he headed for Jamaica, where the Rolling Stones were completing their successful 'Goat's Head Soup'. But while the island itself proved fine for songwriting—holed up in his hotel room, Elton added 20 to the two that were left over from the previous album sessions—the recording facilities were found wanting. The decision was made to cut the losses and return to the Chateau where, in familiar surroundings and with plenty of material to work on, the album grew rapidly into 'Goodbye Yellow Brick Road', the singer's first double vinyl release.

With the rock'n'roll live sound now convincingly duplicated in the studio, Elton and band rocked up a storm on the up-tempo numbers, threw in a selection of trademark ballads, including the title track, and delved back into the classical past for the atmospheric instrumental opener, 'Funeral For A Friend'. This led seamlessly into the rocking 'Love Lies Bleeding', while the lead single was a rocker, too: 'Saturday Night's Alright For Fighting' found Bernie's lyrics satirizing the 'boot boy' culture over a piano-pounding, power-chord backing. The effect was shattering: it's hardly surprising that the Who were called upon to cover the original in the 1991 'Two Rooms' tribute project!

The third single from the album proved to be one of Elton and Bernie's most memorable songs—and, as with many of Bernie's greatest lyrics, its inspiration came from the States. 'Candle In The Wind' told the tragic story of screen goddess Marilyn Monroe, as seen through the eyes of a young fan who had never known her but saw her as 'something more than sexual'. It would, over two decades later, be reworked to pay tribute to another glamorous public figure who died too soon, but in original form it reached Number 11 in Britain.

Surprisingly, Stateside record company executives chose to air its B-side, 'Bennie And The Jets', after a black radio station in Detroit had playlisted it. Their reward was a Number 1 pop hit from what was, in all honesty, not a great song. Nevertheless, this R&B crossover echoed Elton's own youthful listening habits and initial musical direction with Bluesology, and it was to resurface again in 1975 with the non-album single 'Philadelphia Freedom'.

It should by now be apparent that 'Yellow Brick Road' was a diverse double helping with something for everyone—and his fans worldwide lapped it up. Topping the UK album chart as the final Number 1 of the year, it shot past David Cassidy's latest offering, while in the States it remained top of the pile for a full two months, staying in the Top 200 for two whole years. But just to prove that he wasn't taking himself too seriously in the face of such success, Elton flung a seasonal spoonful into the pot with 'Step Into Christmas'/'Ho! Ho! Ho! Who'd Be A Turkey At Christmas'. The A-side occasionally crops up on Xmas compilations, but neither song was going to cause Bing Crosby (or, indeed, Slade, who'd just unleashed their classic 'Merry Xmas Everybody') sleepless nights.

Hollywood Star to Local Hero

September had seen Elton remount the tour treadmill—but in style when, following in the Fab Four's footsteps, he played the gigantic Hollywood Bowl. Blue film star Linda Lovelace introduced him—along with a string of lookalikes, from the Queen and the Pope to Groucho Marx—to the 25,000 crowd as he descended a film-set staircase to a stage where

five grand piano lids spelled E-L-T-O-N. In November he faced a smaller but even more fervent throng when he was acclaimed as the new vice-chairman of Watford Football Club.

The club were his local League side and, in the absence of any sports skills, it was an unexpected thrill to be associated with them. In May the following year, he played a concert at their Vicarage Road ground with friend and fellow football fanatic Rod Stewart to raise much-needed funds, and in time he was to take

Above Charity began at home when, in May 1974, Elton turned Watford FC's Vicarage Road ground into a concert arena. This is the program for an event that was dogged by rain but blessed by the appearance of Rod Stewart, who preferred his tartan scarf to a yellow and black one.

Opposite The piano may not be the most rock'n'roll of instruments, but Elton overcame his early frustration at being "stuck behind a piece of furniture" to prove a worthy successor to the likes of Jerry Lee Lewis and Little Richard.

Left Elton, Rod Stewart, and TV chat-show host Michael Parkinson team up for a good cause—Goaldiggers, a charity intended to give football pitches and sports equipment to deprived kids. Elton was to be a prime mover in Goaldiggers' fund raising efforts.

a major role in the future of the club. Within ten years, the homely Hertfordshire side would reach football's top flight.

Right now, though, it was Elton who was reaching for the stars by touring the States in an airliner named *Starship* fitted out with a piano and a bed. The album he was promoting was his first to be recorded across the Atlantic, at the Caribou ranch of top producer James William Guercio. Just as with 'Honky Chateau', it took the studio's name as its title—but while that particular album had caught Elton and his band on an upward curve, the songs on this effort were uneven, constant touring having left little room for creativity.

Sure, there was the occasional classic—most notably 'Don't Let The Sun Go Down On Me', a harmony-drenched ballad that featured the backing vocal talents of the Beach Boys—but with eight days in which to record fourteen numbers it was bound to feel a little rushed. Yet even 'Elton-by-numbers' was worth lending an ear to: the hard-rocking 'Saturday Night…' theme was developed with 'The Bitch Is Back', its title coming courtesy of Bernie's wife, who coined the phrase when an aggravated Elton entered the room! It would later be adopted as a self-mocking anthem by Tina Turner.

While Elton, who had his own reservations about the album, expected a critical pasting for his latest effort, US reviewers' opinions—in retrospect, at least—were favorable. *Rolling Stone* magazine's Record Guide gave it four stars out of five, while Robert Christgau, in *Rock Albums Of The 1970s*, dubbed him 'a machine' but offered an uncharacteristically generous B+ grade. In any case, a new US recording contract with the MCA label, set to earn Elton a cool $8 million, proved he was cutting the mustard with those in the industry.

A hit machine he may have been, but flesh and blood could only stand so much stress, and an April-May tour of Britain had to be cancelled to let Elton and the band recharge their batteries. When they returned to the States, suitably refreshed, it would not be by Concorde but on the liner SS *France*: quite sensibly, he was going to take his time from now on.

Teaming Up with Lennon

As the American tour continued, Elton's costumes became ever more outlandish—a gorilla suit, a striped bumble-bee top with yellow bobbles, a suit covered with musical notes and the by-now famous selection of outrageous glasses were just a few of the variations. The 44-date itinerary was scheduled to climax at New York's Madison Square Garden on 28 November, Thanksgiving Day. But this was to be a concert with a difference. Earlier in the year, Elton had been invited to play on a couple of tracks destined for a new album by John Lennon. One in particular, 'Whatever Gets You Through The Night', sounded like a hit single to Elton—so much

"I've been a Watford supporter ever since I was a kid living in Northwood....I've seen them in good times and bad times, and I'm not stopping now."

Right The entertainer at home. He exchanged Hercules, his Virginia Water residence, for an Old Windsor mansion as the decade went on.

Below right A pensive Elton faces the press and cameras. As the 1970s wore on, his on-stage ebullience started to transfer to his previously sensitive recordings, though off stage he remained a shy, sensitive character.

Below A pivotal moment in the lives of Elton John and John Lennon—the ex-Beatle's last public appearance before his retirement to become a househusband and father to son Sean. The duo played three songs together on 28 November 1974, including the chart-topping 'Whatever Gets You Through The Night'.

Left Don't shoot me, I'm only the disc jockey. Helped to success by the radio stations, Elton was happy to turn the tables by presenting a show on BBC's Radio 1. Over a decade later he was to receive the radio accolade of appearing as a guest on Radio 4's long-running *Desert Island Discs*.

Bottom left Pandemonium as Elton gets his bizarre dress sense into gear. While the 1980s would see his wardrobe hit new heights of madness and extravagance, his earlier efforts were quite sweet. In 1974 he donned a gorilla suit to invade the stage at an Iggy Pop gig in Atlanta at which he wasn't even playing!

Above Three grand dames of rock—Roderick Stewart, Elton Hercules John, and Paul Gadd, better known these days as Gary Glitter. Although Bernie Taupin socialized with Rod and Gary on the London night-club scene, Elton's private life was generally more low-key.

Above A February 1974 cover story for *Creem*, a US rock magazine that, like many of its rivals, realized that a picture of Elton on the cover in the 1970s guaranteed sales. It was a trait he shared with later cover girl Princess Diana.

so that he struck a bet with the ex-Beatle that if it made Number 1 on the Billboard chart Lennon would come out of retirement to play it with Elton at the Garden.

The pair had cooked up a second collaboration at Caribou since their studio meeting, Lennon repaying the favour by guesting on Elton's cover of his own 'Lucy In The Sky With Diamonds' from 1967's classic 'Sgt Pepper'. This as yet unreleased version was selected as the second song of a three-number solo spot that the couple would do together, Elton giving John the lead but coming in on the choruses. But friendly debate raged over the all-important third choice. Rejecting the obvious 'Imagine', Lennon decided instead to pick "a rock'n'roll song"…not only that, but one from the Beatles rather than his solo repertoire. Elton suggested 'I Saw Her Standing There' - the opening track from the first Beatles album, 'Please Please Me'—momentarily forgetting that it was one of Paul McCartney's songs. Lennon went for it…

And so did the crowd, going wild as the reclusive Lennon came on stage in a dark suit and shades, Fender Telecaster in hand. With a sparkly-flared Elton behind the piano smiling approval and support, the day was a

Right The cover of a Japanese tour program. It was a 1974 Japanese jaunt that caused 'Caribou', the year's major release, to be rushed through in not much more than a week. Yet even this, combined with studio problems, couldn't stop the album rising to the top.

memorable one—and recordings were to surface several years later (albeit in the tragic circumstances following Lennon's shooting). Even more of a cause for celebration, though, was that Yoko Ono, from whom Lennon had been estranged for a number of months, was a surprise visitor backstage—and the day marked the beginning of their reconciliation. Elton's part in that process would be recognized when he was appointed godfather of the couple's son Sean, born in late 1975.

Topping UK and US Charts

Elton's studio version of 'Lucy' was released to the Christmas market and became his third US Number 1 early the following year. A by-now obligatory second album had ended the year in style when 'Greatest Hits' became Elton's most successful long-player to date. It topped both British and American charts, staying at the summit for eleven and ten weeks respectively: perhaps his home country was catching up at last! The songs were those you'd expect, with two exceptions: 'Border Song', which struggled to US Number 92 but won credibility through the Aretha Franklin cover version, appeared on all editions, while 'Bennie And The Jets' took the place of 'Candle In The Wind' on the American issue.

The album's success kept the Rolling Stones' 'It's Only Rock'n'Roll' off the transAtlantic top spot—something Elton must have savoured. Even more significant was the fact that he had cleverly got one step ahead of his horrendous work schedule, using the breather afforded by 'Greatest Hits' to complete his next album of new material. Again Caribou's studios had been the venue, and this time the album was to have a unique concept—it was to be Elton and Bernie's musical autobiography!

"Bernie has the idea of writing about how we met. I have a feeling that it won't be commercial but I never know what is and what isn't."

Left Elton's ever more extravagant dress sense had spread to his off-stage attire, and would lead to him being immortalized by Madame Tussaud's as a life-sized talking model welcoming visitors to the wax museum! Despite the poster doppelganger, this is the real thing.

1975 ★ 1977

While Elton had been gallivanting around the world, Rocket Records had been ticking over quite nicely. Back at home, Kiki Dee had been the first to sell records in any quantity, firstly with the romantic ballad 'Amoureuse' and then with an untypically belting rocker 'I Got The Music In Me', which titled a reasonably successful album. Both singles went Top 20, but she would only go higher with the direct assistance of her 'boss'. Rocket's first US Number 1 would come courtesy of Neil Sedaka, a piano-playing singer-songwriter who'd been an Elton favorite back in the 1960s.

Previous page Elton, Bernie and manager John Reid celebrate the Stateside success of Neil Sedaka, a Brill Building veteran of the early 1960s whose fortunes were revived when he signed to the Rocket label in 1974. Elton would contribute backing vocals to the following year's US chart-topper 'Bad Blood', paying back a stylistic debt audible on his own 'Crocodile Rock'.

Opposite Having transcended the limitations of playing on stage behind a piano and established himself as the natural successor to Jerry Lee Lewis and Little Richard, the late 1970s would see Elton announce his retirement from the live arena. That vow, however, was not to last.

Right The artist formerly known as Cherilyn Sarkasian LaPier meets the one-time Reginald Kenneth Dwight. It was a double act that featured on US TV in 1975, cropped up again when Cher contributed lyrics to the 'Leather Jackets' album in 1986 and finally when she took part in An Audience With Elton John, televised in Britain in late 1997.

Thanks to a great deal of high-profile publicity from his label chief, who made a point of plugging him in every possible radio and TV interview, Neil Sedaka ascended to the top spot with 'Laughter In The Rain' for the first time since 1962.

Elton, meanwhile, was still very much in demand, making an hilarious guest appearance on Cher's US TV show with Bette Midler. He was wheeled on in the disguise of an old man, much to everyone's delight. And if the Elton and Bette double act brought the house down, then Elton and Billie-Jean King proved an even more potent combination. 'Philadelphia Freedom' served not only as an anthem for the former Wimbledon champion's tennis team, but also a homage to the Philly soul sound masterminded by Kenny Gamble and Leon Huff that had recently replaced an ailing Motown as the sound of black America.

The song had been debuted in the dressing room at Denver, near to the Caribou studios, and Billie-Jean was suitably impressed. "Hear the beat?" he said. "That's you when you get mad on the court!" The result, credited to the Elton John Band, only reached a disappointing Number 12 at home but, as might now be expected, it went all the way in the land of sweet soul music to bring him his fourth *Billboard* chart-topper. Such was his standing he was even invited to appear on US TV's *Soul Train*—a rare accolade for a white rock performer.

A Change of Line-Up

Having dedicated a song to Billie-Jean's team, Elton decided to shuffle his own and recruit a brand-new band. Retaining Davey Johnstone from his long-time backing trio, he not only replaced the faithful rhythm section of Nigel and Dee (with Roger Pope and American Kenny Passarelli) but added an extra guitar in Caleb Quaye and a keyboardist/arranger in James Newton Howard. Elton agreed firing such close friends was "an impossible situation" but stressed the positive: "I've always wanted to be part of a good driving rock'n'roll band. The old band used to rattle on—I want to chug rather than race." A change of pace, then, was clearly on the cards…but not before the public had digested the last long-player from the

Right Los Angeles declared 21 November 1975 Elton John Day, as the performer was honored with his very own star on Hollywood's celebrated Walk of Fame. He accepted the accolade dressed in a spangly white suit and bowler hat, flying out the entire Rocket London office, plus sundry pals, to share in the glory.

Right Pounding the 'eighty eights' in inimitable fashion. Elton would inevitably restrict himself to piano on stage, latterly employing a second keyboard player (American James Newton Howard in the band he recruited in 1975) to add textures on organ and synthesizer.

Right Elton is the meat in the sandwich as two noted pickers, Doobie Brother Jeff 'Skunk' Baxter and Elton's own guitarist Davey Johnstone, exchange notes. Recruited in 1972, Johnstone would still be working with the piano-player 25 years later—a considerable achievement in an ever-changing band line-up.

Center right Elton and Billie-Jean King, the former Wimbledon tennis champion who has long been a friend. He wrote the US chart-topping 'Philadelphia Freedom' to celebrate her tennis team, while the 1990s would see her return the favor by helping him set up pro-celebrity tournaments to raise funds for his AIDS foundation.

ELTON JOHN

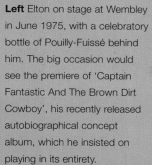

Left Elton on stage at Wembley in June 1975, with a celebratory bottle of Pouilly-Fuissé behind him. The big occasion would see the premiere of 'Captain Fantastic And The Brown Dirt Cowboy', his recently released autobiographical concept album, which he insisted on playing in its entirety.

Below Elton with new band guitarist Caleb Quaye. Their association dated back to the early days when a teenage Quaye was studio manager at DJM. They also played together briefly in Bluesology. He'd meanwhile led his own band called Hookfoot, from which Elton had also recruited drummer Roger Pope.

Above A program for the all-star concert at Wembley on 21 June 1975 which gave fans their first chance to see his new band with whom he'd been rehearsing in Holland for much of the month. Elton's chums the Beach Boys are given special prominence in a program as elaborately designed as any of his record sleeves.

Below A tour program from 1976 shows that Elton's part in the film *Tommy* had been immortalized by the creation of a new pinball table. 'Bally salutes Captain Fantastic' runs the legend as Elton poses proudly. The 'Louder than Concorde but not quite as pretty' tour slogan was apparently inspired by a remark from Princess Margaret.

old team. 'Captain Fantastic And The Brown Dirt Cowboy' was a real return to form after 'Caribou'. According to producer Gus Dudgeon, "It was obviously going to be something special from the moment we first heard the songs." Captain Fantastic, of course, was Elton, while Taupin's title derived from his rural upbringing and the long-standing fascination with the Wild West that had so often come out in his lyrics.

Now familiar with the Caribou studios (there had been significant production problems to overcome first time round), Dudgeon recorded it "flat" and "did all the work in the mix." Also, with the song sequence known from the outset, everything was worked on in order, each song linking perfectly with the next. Percussionist Ray Cooper was also on board and, like Johnstone, he would survive the post-recording personnel changes.

The resulting album became the first ever in US chart history to enter *Billboard*'s listing at the very top, elbowing aside disco kings Earth Wind and Fire with almost contemptuous ease. In Britain, black music held its own, and it was kept off the top by 'The Best Of The Stylistics'. Undeterred, Elton chose to play the album in its entirety when he returned to home turf for an outdoor festival-style gig at Wembley Stadium—just up the road from his childhood stamping ground of Pinner—on 21 June. A stellar supporting cast, hand-picked by Elton himself, included the Eagles, the Beach Boys, Joe Walsh, Rufus, and Rocket signings Stackridge.

Whether it was wise or not to plug his new album rather than more traditional fare (reports suggest a proportion of the audience left early), dyed-in-the-wool Eltonophiles gave the album their unreserved thumbs-up. The single 'Someone Saved My Life Tonight', referring to his botched suicide attempt during the Linda Woodrow affair, made a disappointing Number 22 in Britain, although US fans hoisted it into the Top 5. And rightly so, since it richly deserved to be up there among his great ballads with the similarly-paced 'Don't Let The Sun Go Down On Me'.

As it turned out, this was to be his pen-ultimate album for DJM—and had it been his swan song that would indeed have been fitting. The expensive album packaging included two books of lyrics and memorabilia and a poster, combining with a gatefold sleeve to create something quite special, a "thank you" to long-time fans that remains unique in his body of recorded work to date.

Elton and Bernie were so prolific they were even able to give a couple of songs away to friends Ringo Starr ('Snookeroo', which appeared on his album 'Goodnight Vienna') and Rod Stewart ('Let Me Be Your Car', on 1974's 'Smiler'). Elton himself was given a hit by Pete Townshend, who invited him to play the Pinball Wizard in Ken Russell's big-screen adaptation of the rock opera 'Tommy'. The oversized boots became yet another stage prop, while the character's theme tune—the acoustic guitar replaced by cascading keyboards—gave him a Number 7 UK hit.

"It was obviously going to be something special from the moment we first heard the songs"

Above The Acid Queen meets the Pinball Wizard at the premier of the film version of the Who's *Tommy*. Tina Turner would later adopt 'The Bitch Is Back' from 'Caribou' as her tongue-in-cheek theme song as she completed a spectacular career renaissance in the 1980s.

Left The Pinball Wizard in action. The trademark oversize boots were kept as a memento, used in the 'Nikita' video in 1985 and eventually sold off in one of the auctions of memorabilia that accompanied Elton's late-1980s attempts to get his life back on track and divest himself of the excesses of the past.

Right Woodside, Elton's UK hideaway in Old Windsor since moving from Hercules in early 1976. The 1990s have seen him maintain a second home in Atlanta, Georgia, where in contrast to this mansion he occupies the upper floors of a tower block, but he still prizes his British home for the last two decades.

Below right In an off-stage moment, Elton displays rather unusual dress sense in a denim outfit plastered with every conceivable kind of badge, from Ban the Bomb to Spiro Agnew.

Below Two record-breaking concerts at Los Angeles' Dodger Stadium at the end of November 1975 brought the West Of The Rockies tour to a suitably rousing climax. Attired in a sequin-augmented Dodgers baseball uniform, he was the first rock act to play the 50,000-capacity venue since the Beatles in 1966.

NEARLY FAMOUS

Left Although as unalike as chalk and cheese, Elton and Cliff Richard were brought up in neighboring north London suburbs (Cliff in Enfield). Elton, nearly seven years the junior of the 'Peter Pan of Pop', gave him a helping hand to Stateside success with the Rocket-released album 'I'm Nearly Famous'.

Below left The artist relaxes at home. The album-tour-album schedule he'd kept up since his first hit had left little time to lounge around, yet the quality of his output, often two albums a year, remained commendably high.

Below Elton with the victorious Watford FC team which won the Fourth Division championship in 1978. In 1997 his return as chairman after an absence of several years saw the team at the top of the Second Division and bidding to recapture former glories under reinstalled manager Graham Taylor.

Captain Fantastic...

...And The Brown Dirt Cowboy

Musicians Elton John (keyboards, vocals), Dee Murray (bass), Nigel Olsson (drums), Davey Johnstone (guitar), Ray Cooper (percussion) David Hentschel (synthesizer) • **Recorded at** Caribou Studios, Colorado • **Top 20 hit singles** 'Someone Saved My Life Tonight' (US 4, UK 22) • **Unusual fact** The specially commissioned cover art was contributed by Alan Aldridge, best known for his children's book Butterfly Ball • **Track listing** Captain Fantastic And The Brown Dirt Cowboy • Tower Of Babel • Bitter Fingers • Tell Me When The Whistle Blows • Someone Saved My Life Tonight • (Gotta Get A) Meal Ticket • Better Off Dead • Writing • We All Fall In Love Sometimes • Curtains • **Commentary** Hitherto, Bernie Taupin's lyrics had been penned without consultation with his music-writing partner. This time was different, as they traced the course of their relationship through good times and bad. The latter was covered in 'Someone Saved My Life Tonight', dedicated to Long John Baldry, whose advice at a crucial time had been appreciated • The affection in which Elton and Bernie held each other (and their fans reciprocated) shone through in this uniquely personal package of songs. In terms of the actual packaging, Rocket Records paid for the cover art after DJM's budget was exceeded—but critics and purchasers alike raved at the result • **Elsewhere in 1975...** Dr Feelgood release 'Down By The Jetty' • Stardust premieres in Boston • T-Bone Walker and Tim Buckley pass away • Tommy Bolin replaces Ritchie Blackmore in Deep Purple • Sonny and Cher are divorced • Rod Stewart 'sails' to Number 1 • Queen release 'Bohemian Rhapsody' • The Sex Pistols play their first gig at a London college

Released March 1975

Chart Position UK 2

Chart Position US 1 (7 weeks)

Producer Gus Dudgeon

June found him back in the States, jamming with the Eagles and the Doobie Brothers in Oakland, California. The US tour on which he was embarking was to climax with two shows at LA's Dodger Stadium in October, the same month he was awarded a star on Hollywood's Walk of Fame. He claimed accepting the honor was "more nerve-wracking than a concert", though both events were accolades—the last rock act to have played the legendary Dodger venue being the Beatles back in 1966.

The tour as a whole grossed in excess of $2.2 million, and as the last notes died away his doctors ordered a dose of rest and recuperation. The next four months were to be spent in the Barbados sun…

Over-shadowed

The final album for DJM, 'Rock Of The Westies', had been released in October. Its title, a pun on 'West of the Rockies', had replaced the original 'Bottled And Brained'—and the recording almost inevitably paled by comparison with 'Captain Fantastic', which Elton had dubbed "the first album about me." This, though, was the first with the new band and, while there should have been a rock edge to proceedings thanks to the twin-guitar attack of Johnstone and Quaye, too many tracks were, as Elton might have put it, "typical chuggers." Some suggested that a personality clash between Elton's guitarist and other members had resulted in him not being as prominent as usual: producer Dudgeon recalls "some weirdness going on", and confessed to a mistake of his own.

Patti LaBelle, whose BlueBelles Elton had once backed as a member of Bluesology, had been delighted to pop into the studios with

"With two albums a year, and chart-toppers at that, the royalty cheques had been landing thick and fast on the doormat of Hercules"

her current companions, Sarah Dash and Nona Hendryx, and repay the debt by singing the backing on the opening medley of 'Yell Help', 'Wednesday Night', and 'Ugly'. So far, so good…but Dudgeon had neglected to record their parts on the last chorus. His solution: "I made myself an enormous joint, walked into the studio and imitated LaBelle…nobody's spotted it, not even Elton!"

Whatever the artistic reservations, no-one could doubt 'Rock Of The Westies' had made history. By entering the US chart at Number 1, it had made Elton John the first and only artist to score two such singles in a calendar year. As the Who's Pete Townshend said, "Elton could shit bricks and people would go out and buy them." Back home, as punk rock monopolized the headlines, the album reached Number 5. Elton's verdict? "It probably doesn't have much depth to it, but I kinda like it."

The album's first single, 'Island Girl', gave him his fifth US Number 1 in November—and ironically gave him the chance to replace his 'protégé', Neil Sedaka, who'd occupied the spot with 'Bad Blood' for the previous three weeks. Elton had sung (uncredited) backing vocals on that song, so by stretching a point could claim a month's residency at the top!

With two albums a year, and chart-toppers at that, the royalty checks had been landing thick and fast on the doormat of Hercules—so the next step for Elton John was to invest in even more substantial bricks and mortar. Never mind that he was on tour for most of the year: 'Woodside', a mansion in Old Windsor, would be the place he would henceforth call home. In

Above Elton converses with Queen frontman Freddie Mercury at the Cliff Richard album party. The two master showmen would share the glory of Live Aid on the Wembley stage in 1985, but in 1992 Elton would tread that stage with Axl Rose as they mourned Mercury's loss to AIDS.

fact, the call of his native land was to become significantly greater when, at the end of the 1976-77 football season, he upgraded his status at Watford Football Club from vice-chairman to chairman. He'd earlier told *Playboy* magazine his ambition was to retire and concentrate on that job—though few yet took him at his word.

Rocket on the Rise

With his DJM contract now fulfilled, Elton was able to become a Rocket *artiste* at last. The label would have two notable successes in 1976—one involving him, the other a repeat of the Neil Sedaka story. Cliff Richard had never made a name for himself in the States, where he was regarded rightly or wrongly as an Elvis Presley clone. By the 1970s, he was producing less derivative fare and seemed ripe for a Stateside relaunch. Elton signed him up to Rocket and, while the first attempt 'Miss You Nights' failed to score, 'Devil Woman'— a highly contemporary and infectious single that could have been Daryl Hall at his best— gave him the breakthrough…whereupon his original label, Capitol, took him back!

Opposite Hamming it up on stage in uncharacteristically businesslike tracksuit bottoms. 'Captain Fantastic' was arguably an album that worked better in recorded form than live. But the ballad 'Someone Saved My Life Tonight' remained an enduring stage favorite.

Right Elton's usually cordial relationship with the Royals was inadvertently strained by this May 1977 meeting with Princess Alexandra at a charity concert. He publicly repeated her question as to whether he took cocaine to reporters, breaking protocol. The answer, he emphasized while apologizing through the media, was no… though he would admit to having indulged when in 'clean and repentant' mode in the 1990s.

Far right In a spectacular crescendo that must have satisfied Elton's sense of the theatrical, the snow falls and the lights sparkle in a stage scene firmly rooted in cabaret and the circus.

Right Involvement in soccer gave Elton the chance to rub shoulders with some of his sporting idols who, in their turn, were often his fans. Northern Ireland international George Best, whose finest hours in a Manchester United shirt coincided with Elton's debut as a recording artist, was one of these. By the time of the photo, their careers had moved in different directions (Best was with Los Angeles Aztecs) and Elton was the superstar.

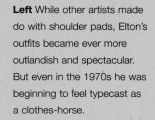

Left While other artists made do with shoulder pads, Elton's outfits became ever more outlandish and spectacular. But even in the 1970s he was beginning to feel typecast as a clothes-horse.

Above Elton's 1977 tour was supported by China, the band formed by guitarist Davey Johnstone and featuring Jo Partridge (guitar), James Newton Howard (keyboards), Dennis Conway (drums) and Cooker Lo Presti (bass). Elton and Clive Franks would co-produce the band's eponymous Rocket Records album, but it made little commercial impact.

Left Kiss and make up? Elton and US heavy metal glam-rockers Kiss had little in common but a sense of showmanship and a vaultful of platinum disks, but were happy to share the spotlight in this photo call. Gene Simmons would at one point date Elton's pal Cher, so at least there was a possible topic of conversation!

Above Kiki Dee, alias Bradford-born Pauline Matthews, looked set for success when America's mighty Motown signed her. But her career had hit the doldrums in the early 1970s before Elton signed her to Rocket—and he stepped in again to duet with her to chart-topping effect in 1976. The pairing would be repeated frequently in concert and, memorably, at 1985's Live Aid.

The other success was even dearer to Elton's heart, as it won him his very first UK Number 1 single. The song was 'Don't Go Breaking My Heart', which he performed as a duet with the effervescent Kiki Dee, whose chart career had bottomed out after her initial success.

The song that won Elton his much-coveted Number 1 (having got closest with 1972's 'Rocket Man') had a fascinating genesis. Elton recorded his side of the duet at Eastern Sound studios in Toronto, Canada, where he'd put together his next long-player, while Kiki added her vocal after the tape had been flown back to London, Gus Dudgeon again presiding. Fittingly, in view of its transatlantic origins, the song topped the charts on both sides of the ocean, also promoting Elton in several markets he'd previously failed to penetrate. Given their respective schedules, it's not surprising the duo didn't get round to recording a follow-up,

the Motown classic 'Loving You Is Sweeter Than Ever', until 1981! However, the success of 'Don't Go Breaking My Heart' enabled Elton to tell *Rolling Stone* magazine he'd "achieved all my childhood dreams."

Taupin and John, for some obscure reason, had credited themselves as songwriters under the *noms de disque* of Anne Orson/Carte Blanche (say it aloud if you don't get the joke!). Earlier in the year, DJM had been given *carte blanche* to release a final Elton album—the live 'Here And There', made up of recordings made in London and New York in 1974. Inevitably, it made the US Top 5 and the UK Top 10.

Accolades, awards, and commendations had showered Elton John with monotonous regularity over the past few years, but three that took place in 1976 deserve special mention. The legendary Madame Tussaud's waxwork museum in Baker Street broke with tradition and decided to immortalize him in wax form—the first rock star to be granted that signal honor—and he received an invitation to perform on TV's *Muppet Show*, where Miss Piggy assumed the Kiki Dee role as if to the manner born. Lastly, but not least, he became the first rock star to enter Madison Square Garden's Hall of Fame.

Feeling the Pressure

The pressures of fame were by now immense, especially in America, which had long since adopted him as one of their own. "I don't want to end up my life like Elvis," he told *Rolling Stone* magazine. "I went to an amusement park while on tour and 13 people surrounded me for protection: I felt like the Pope." Like close friend John Lennon, he'd soon decide the way to deal with this was to opt out of the rock'n'roll circus—temporarily, at least.

Curiously, Elton's first album for his own label, 'Blue Moves', was the first since 'Madman' not to hit the US top spot. But every cloud has a silver lining, and, with the system of platinum records having just been instigated, this was his first album to turn that particular shade of precious metal, with sales of two million copies.

Accountable to no-one but himself, Elton had spared no expense. The double album, containing no fewer than three instrumentals, was heavily arranged and orchestrated (not only by James Newton Howard but also by old friend Paul Buckmaster) and included guest musicians of the caliber of Crosby and Nash, the Brecker Brothers, Toni Tennille, and Beach Boy Bruce Johnston.

The single 'Sorry Seems To Be The Hardest Word' deserved its place in both the charts and the pantheon of Elton and Bernie's best ballads,

but 'Crazy Water' and 'Bite Your Lip (Get Up And Dance)' were less successful single follow-ups. The huge swings in musical mood, from the gospel chorus of 'Bite Your Lip' to the soothing harmonies of 'Chameleon', could not disguise the downbeat lyrical tone of the album, but if Bernie Taupin's lyrics were a little on the dark side (Elton described them as "real desperate") it was hardly surprising: his marriage was suffering some stresses and strains.

Whether Elton consciously decided to go for something more upbeat in the future can't be said for certain, but the pair's present lifestyles—Elton at home with Watford, Bernie hanging out with the West Coast rock'n'roll élite—were as disparate as they'd ever been. A temporary split, then, was very much on the cards.

Below "Everybody knows I'm desperately in love with Miss Piggy," declared Elton before making a guest appearance on *The Muppet Show* to plug the Number 1 'Don't Go Breaking My Heart'. His regular duet partner Kiki Dee was prepared to let the object of Elton's affections take her place "just this once."

"An interview with *Rolling Stone* reporter Cliff Jahr made public what pop insiders had suspected for some while: that Elton John was 'bisexual'"

Right Mod revivalists the Lambrettas strike a suitably Who-like pose as they look for lasting success on Rocket. Sadly, it was not to be and they, as well as the label, would dwindle into obscurity after 'Poison Ivy' gave them a Number 7 hit in early 1980. In truth, Elton was too busy with his own career to push Rocket Records to the heights.

As for Elton's own personal life, an interview with *Rolling Stone* reporter Cliff Jahr made public what pop insiders had suspected for some while: that he was 'bisexual'. No scandal, no front-page headlines—these were the days when the broadsheets, not the tabloids, ruled Fleet Street. Of more concern to Elton at this point than his sexual revelation was the fact that Rocket had lost its upward momentum. Gus Dudgeon had resigned, the suggestion being that he'd had less than a free hand in selecting artists to sign: Dave Edmunds, one of his reported choices, was picked up by Led Zeppelin's label, SwanSong, and immediately started a run of successful hit singles. Not bad for a has-been... Conversely, Dudgeon's successor signed a more youthful, 'with-it' bunch of Mod revivalists known as the Lambrettas whose run of Top 40 hits would extend to just two, most notably a cover of the Coasters' R&B classic 'Poison Ivy'.

Judie Tzuke, a singer-songwriter with skills that put her in the Joan Armatrading class, was potentially a more promising signing. Unfortunately, the British music scene was turning away from such class acts to women in rock like Siouxsie and X-Ray Spex's Poly Styrene, and 'Stay With Me Till Dawn' was to remain her sole singles success. After her departure, it was inevitable Rocket would become a conduit for its owner's recordings rather than, as had been hoped, something more.

The success of 'Bennie And The Jets' and 'Philadelphia Freedom' suggested Elton could profit from following a more black-influenced direction. Certainly, the punk-infested British singles charts offered little solace for a singer-songwriter, and his Stateside audience was still strong, despite 'Blue Moves' 'only' reaching Number 3 (the same position as at home).

Accordingly, the decision was made to do some recording with noted soul producer Thom Bell, whose previous charges had included the Detroit Spinners and the Stylistics. The pair didn't hit it off, though a comment by Bell was to have a lasting effect on him.

"You sing too high and you don't use your lower register properly" was the advice Bell gave—and though Elton didn't care much to be told this at the time, he'd later acknowledge it to be "absolutely correct...since then, I've much more range in my voice." It was at this point, he has since said, that he started enjoying singing as much as playing the piano—so take a bow Mr Bell! No album emerged from their collaboration, but enough material was cut for a 'Thom Bell Sessions' EP, headed by 'Mama Can't Buy You Love' and eventually released in 1979: to no-one's surprise, it was better received in the States than at home.

No More Tours

Elton's live work schedule had been punishing, so it seemed sensible, given his commitments to Watford FC, that he should call a halt to the treadmill and, while continuing to record, cut out the grueling world tours that had twice seen him collapse on stage. He chose to make this announcement while on stage at Wembley Arena, playing a charity gala.

He ended 1977 with another appearance on *Top Of The Pops*—this time as the host. It's unlikely the guests included shock-rocker Alice Cooper, but he was to be Bernie's next port of call, as Captain Fantastic and the Brown Dirt Cowboy took a break from each other's musical company. For the first time since his earliest recordings, Elton was venturing into the studio without the lyrical assistance of his friend and ally. The results looked set to be interesting...

Above Singer-songwriter Judie Tzuke was at the right place at the wrong time. Elton's patronage guaranteed her attention, but the late 1970s was more concerned with anarchy than affection and her July 1979 hit 'Stay With Me Till Dawn' plus three chart albums would prove the sum of her stay on Rocket. She was still active in the 1990s, releasing records on her own indie label.

wilderness
years

The break with Bernie Taupin coincided with

what Elton fans would term 'the wilderness years'—a time when the singer not only seemed to lose his way musically but his commercial standing, for so long unquestioned, especially in the States, was to take a hammering. It was amazing, in retrospect, how long the salad days had lasted: come disco, punk, or any trend you cared to mention, Elton had weathered the storm. Yet people grow older, and popular music becomes less important in the face of mortgages, diapers, and mid-life crises. Like any other artist with longevity, Elton would have to reach a new generation of admirers to compensate for the natural drop-off in his core fanbase.

Previous page Elton remained a recognizable public figure no matter how his commercial fortunes waxed and waned. Here he runs the gauntlet of autograph hunters. The cap was one of many attempts to disguise his thinning thatch. "It didn't happen to the rest of my family…it must have been because I dyed my hair a lot," he'd reveal to *Playboy* in 1976, adding that he was seriously considering a transplant.

Right Alice Cooper was the next recipient of Bernie Taupin's lyrical talents after splitting with Elton. His lyrics for Cooper's 1978 effort 'From The Inside' told of the singer's struggle against drink and drugs—far more specific and intimate than his writing for Elton would ever get, even though his oldest friend would encounter similar serious problems.

Opposite As Elton entered the 1980s, his costumes became ever more elaborate and expensive. This one, unveiled for the 1982 tour, was splashed over the *Daily Mirror* under the banner headline 'The Gay Hussar!', illustrating both Elton's newsworthiness and the tabloids' obsessive fascination with his sexuality.

His first steps toward that end would be taken in partnership with Gary Osborne, a former jingle writer who'd found limited fame with songwriting partner Paul Vigrass. His connection with Elton and Rocket came about through Kiki Dee's debut hit, 'Amoureuse', for which he'd provided new English lyrics. As Elton's main writing partner in the forthcoming months, he contributed to all but one of the tracks on December 1978's 'A Single Man'—but he had much to live up to.

Elton claims the idea of him and Bernie taking a sabbatical from each other was "a misconception…there was no falling out." As luck would have it, though, Bernie's first album for an outside singer, the aforementioned Alice Cooper's 'From The Inside', coincided with the new release. While few would compare the piano man from Pinner with shock-rocker Vince Furnier (Alice's real name), there was an element of competition that the press were quick to play up.

The intriguingly titled 'A Single Man' was Elton's first new album for two years—and ironically, with all eyes (and ears) on his new lyricist, its biggest track would be an instrumental. 'Song For Guy' was inspired by the death of Guy Burchett, a Rocket Records

messenger killed in a road accident. A haunting piano tune, it reached Number 4 as a single, while the parent album made a promising 8 in Britain and 15 in the States.

An Undeniable Hit

The previous single but one, 'Ego' (the last for now to boast a Taupin lyric), had only reached Number 34 on both sides of the Atlantic and its relative lack of success had immediately preceded a public attack by Elton on the "highly inaccurate" nature of the BBC chart. Pundits, of course, smelled sour grapes, but 'Guy' proved a *bona fide* hit regardless of any data-collecting imperfections. (US charts are collated on a mixture of sales and airplay, and a similar system would probably have benefited Elton had it operated in Britain.)

It was even rumored that it could have been a chart-topper had Phonogram, Rocket's newly appointed distributor, not put their might behind the Village People's 'YMCA' in the capacity-squeezed run-up to Christmas.

The album, musically workmanlike, was most remarkable for its packaging, depicting Elton standing outside Windsor Castle on the outer sleeve and behind the wheel of a gleaming sports car on the inner gatefold.

A Single Man

Musicians Elton John (keyboards, vocals), Clive Franks (percussion, vocals), Ray Cooper (percussion), Pat Halcox (trumpet), Stevie Lange (vocals), Joanne Stone (vocals), Paul Buckmaster (cello), John Crocker (woodwinds), Herbie Flowers (bass), Davey Johnstone (guitar, vocals), Chris Thompson (vocals), Jim Shepherd (trombone), Henry Lowther (trumpet), Gary Osborne (vocals), Tim Renwick (guitar), Steve Holly (drums) • **Recorded at** Mill Studios, Cookham, Berkshire • **Top 20 hit singles** Part-Time Love (UK 15, US 22), Song For Guy (UK 4) • **Unusual fact** This was the first Elton album to be distributed by Phonogram, the record company that (then known as Philips) had issued his first singles as part of Bluesology • **Track listing** Shine On Through • Return To Paradise • I Don't Care • Big Dipper • It Ain't Gonna Be Easy • Part-Time Love • Georgia • Shooting Star • Madness • Reverie • Song For Guy • **Commentary** Having dispensed—temporarily, at least—with specs in favor of contact lenses, Elton's fortunes looked decidedly rosier with the healthy performance of this album. Although lacking Bernie Taupin's lyrical bite, Gary Osborne had come up with his best shots, which Elton graced with an above average selection of melodies. The pick of the bunch, however, was reserved for the closing instrumental, which would become a major hit single • This all came as light relief after the doom and gloom-laden 'Blue Moves', although the earlier album's status has grown over time. Yet such is the glossy optimism evident here, with massed backing vocals, horns, and all manner of musical gizmos, that long-time producer Gus Dudgeon is hardly missed. The ideal Christmas record in every respect • **Elsewhere in 1978...** The Sex Pistols undertake their first US tour, then split up • The Rutles' spoof TV Beatles documentary *All You Need Is Cash* airs in the US • Kate Bush enjoys her first hit with 'Wuthering Heights' • Bob Dylan sells 90,000 Wembley tickets in eight hours • Travolta and Newton-John's *Grease* anthem 'You're The One That I Want' tops the UK chart • Heavy metal hopefuls Van Halen sign to Warner Brothers • 10CC top the charts with 'Dreadlock Holiday' • Fairport Convention singer Sandy Denny suffers a fatal fall down stairs

Released October 1978

Chart Position UK 8

Chart Position US 15

Producer Elton John/ Clive Franks

Among the musician credits lurked the Watford FC first team squad, who'd been persuaded to add *en masse* backing vocals to 'Georgia' and 'Big Dipper': heaven knows what the Americans made of it all! And with the jaunty 'Part Time Love' having cracked the punk-filled Top 30 for the first time in two years as its first single, it seemed his fortunes were on the up once more. Sure enough, the announcement soon came that, after an 18-month retirement, Elton was to go back on the road again.

He'd already made tentative steps stageward, jamming with new wavers Lene Lovich, Wreckless Eric and company on the Stiff Records tour in Hemel Hempstead in November, and joining old stager Eric Clapton at Guildford's Civic Hall the following month. His own return to the spotlight took place in February 1979 in Stockholm with the start of the 'Single Man' tour, in which he appropriately performed solo—with the notable exception of percussionist Ray Cooper!

A short British jaunt followed, and then another piece of history when he became the first Western pop star to

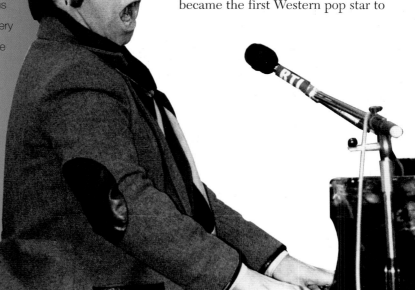

tour the USSR. A film crew followed piano-man and percussionist around as they played four concerts in Moscow and a similar number in Leningrad—and, as the tabloids back home proclaimed the coming of 'Elton John Super-czar', the pleasure he evidently gave the music-starved citizens of those two cities struck home.

"It was one of the most memorable and happy tours I've been on," beamed an invigorated Elton, adding: "The hospitality was tremendous, the only negative experience two or three vodka hangovers." His mother and stepfather were there to witness the triumph at first hand, as well as enjoying a spot of sightseeing with the off-duty czar—sorry, star—of the show. And what a show it was: the flower-strewn stage he left after climaxing his set with a rumbustious cover of the Beatles' 'Back In The USSR' attested to the fact that this was most definitely a case of to Russia with love.

Back on the Pitch

At home, Watford Football Club had been making great strides under boss Graham Taylor, whom Elton had been instrumental in recruiting back in 1977. On the eve of his departure, a delighted chairman presented his manager with a gold disk he'd been awarded for 'A Single Man' to celebrate a season in which the club rose from the Third to the Second Division (in the days before the Premier League, this was the last step to the top flight). Watford had also enjoyed a giant-killing League Cup run that ended just one round short of Wembley when they lost to Nottingham Forest, ironically the team Roy Dwight had once played for.

Having thrown off his vodka hangover, it was time for the singer to give the public yet another surprise. Most pop stars, after making an initial impression, become somewhat run of the mill

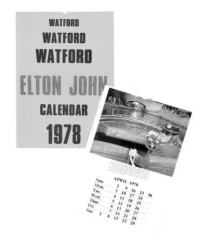

Above Elton lent all his efforts to boosting Watford's fortunes and finances, this 1978 calendar being just one example.

Below left Despite the album title 'A Single Man', Elton rarely went out as a totally solo act. For his return to live work in Russia, he elected to play with percussionist Ray Cooper, who has featured in many different band line-ups. On one tour, a life-sized mannequin took Ray's place while he was recovering from illness.

Opposite Elton vigorously promoted 'A Single Man', and is pictured here in France giving his all. The lettering on the mike suggests that this performance was being considered for broadcast by Radio Luxembourg.

Right Elton displays his lifelong affection for Disney by taking on the character of Donald Duck. He's also been known to perform as Minnie Mouse, while a further brush with Walt's animal kingdom would come in 1994 when he re-entered the soundtrack world.

Far right Elton looks as if he's given his all here. There were a number of on-stage collapses over the years as he continued to push himself to the limits. In September 1979, for instance, flu forced him to take a break at Hollywood's Universal Amphitheatre. He was back within ten minutes and completed a three-hour show.

Right Guitar lessons from Davey Johnstone, his ever-loyal guitarist. It's perhaps surprising Johnstone hasn't taken more of a part in the writing process over a quarter-century, but to date he has contributed to just one song—the 1983 hit single 'I Guess That's Why They Call It The Blues'.

Left The wide-brimmed hat would be Elton's on and off-stage standby in the 1980s, replacing the flat cap of the previous decade. Though he toted a Queen Mary-style toque at Live Aid, the hat would remain a fixture until the late-1980s adoption of the Nehru-style forage cap, which remains popular today. By the 1990s however, transplants had resulted in a thicker head of hair than previously.

Below Elton has shared a microphone with many *artistes* in his time, but his 1977 single 'The Goaldigger Song', recorded with soccer pundit Jimmy Hill (pictured), commentator Brian Moore, and comedian Eric Morecambe for charity, would become his hardest-to-find record. Only 500 copies were pressed, although whether the result is worth the price it commands is debatable.

as time goes by—yet as he celebrated his first decade as a recording artist, Elton was proving anything but predictable. His fans had had to adjust to a new band, retirement, and then to the new double act with Ray Cooper in quick succession, but his next move was even more unprecedented. Recorded in Nice, Munich, Los Angeles, and Hollywood in August and rush-released the following month, 'Victim Of Love' was a one-off—the only Elton John album with no songwriting input from the man himself.

He'd elected to put himself in the hands of Pete Bellotte, best known as sidekick of Eurodisco producer Giorgio Moroder. At least the result wasn't the worst case scenario—Elton John sings Donna Summer—but was an undistinguished affair despite the presence among the backing musicians of such luminaries as Toto guitarist Steve Lukather and virtuoso

Below New-wave bard and bass-player Tom Robinson had enjoyed a difficult relationship with the Kinks' Ray Davies, after signing to his record label as part of Café Society—but was a band leader with hit records behind him by the time he collaborated with Elton. The duo's relatively few co-compositions appeared on albums dominated by the lyrics of Gary Osborne who had taken the place of Bernie Taupin as Elton's regular writing partner.

young bassist Marcus Miller. For the first time, Elton had allowed himself to be led by trends rather than rising above them, and the public proved as unimpressed as the critics. It stalled one place outside the UK Top 40 to give him his first album 'failure' since 1971; US fans, usually so loyal, sent it just six places higher. Singles-wise, the title track was a minor US hit, while a version of Chuck Berry's classic 'Johnny B Goode', sank like a stone: it was time for a rethink.

A New Decade

The year of 1980 dawned with a *Daily Express* report that Elton's mum had bought a house near Brighton, and would no longer be housekeeping at his mansion. He was a big boy now, and that maturity—as well as his prolific album output—was reflected in the title of his next album, '21 At 33'. Two Taupin songs were included: 'Two Rooms At The End Of The World', whose lyrics looked back fondly at their long-distance writing relationship, and 'White Lady White Powder'. The latter, which featured backing vocals from the Eagles, lamented the cocaine-snorting LA lifestyle that Taupin was observing at close quarters.

Though the album contained a big US hit single (Number 3) in 'Little Jeannie', one of three songs co-penned with Gary Osborne, Elton had explored other writing partnerships. The fruits of two such collaborations, with new-waver Tom Robinson (of 'Glad To Be Gay' fame) and Rocket labelmate Judie Tzuke, appeared here. Further John-Robinson songs would appear on the following year's 'The Fox'.

For pop fans, the year of 1980 would be remembered with sorrow as that in which John Lennon was shot. Elton was understandably devastated by news of the ex-Beatle's death,

"For pop fans, the year of 1980 would be remembered with sorrow as that in which John Lennon was shot"

which he heard of after landing at Melbourne, Australia, on a flight from Brisbane. The airliner was cleared of everyone but Elton's party before a weeping John Reid imparted the sad truth. Reaching his hotel, Elton immediately phoned Yoko Ono, and, while touring commitments prevented him being at the funeral, he arranged a service at a local cathedral where he "said good-bye" to a dear friend in his own way.

A live recording of 'I Saw Her Standing There' was released in tribute by DJM (though one of the tracks it contained had already been an Elton B-side). He was to create a more lasting statement in the later 'Empty Garden'. The time they'd shared the Madison Square Garden stage remained Lennon's last live performance: dreams of a comeback tour to follow the 'Double Fantasy' album had been ended by Mark Chapman's bullets.

In 1981 Elton changed labels in the US from MCA to Geffen, while remaining on Rocket at home. It was an interesting move, following John Lennon's signing with David Geffen, the man behind the Eagles' success. MCA had apparently wanted to sign him for the whole world if they were to justify coming up with as generous a deal as 1974's $8 million had been, and that was unacceptable to both Elton and manager Reid.

Geffen was unable to match the money MCA would have paid, but could offer his own sure touch, track record, and flair in marketing. The first fruit of the new partnership was 'The Fox', produced by Chris Thomas, whose stock was high from associations with the Sex Pistols and the Pretenders. While Elton was hardly going

to become a punk overnight (save for the occasional Mohican hairpiece, for stage use only), the result was unimpressive by his own high standards. The use of Tom Robinson and Gary Osborne alongside Taupin gave an unfocussed result, as reflected by the performance of singles 'Nobody Wins' and 'Just Like Belgium', both of which failed to chart in Britain.

If Elton was considered just a little 'establishment' in a year when Adam and the Ants were ruling the charts and airwaves with their jungle rhythms, then perhaps that wasn't totally surprising. After all, he could claim to be the Royal Family's favorite pop star! With the 21st birthday of Prince Andrew due in February 1981, a summons was issued requesting the pianist's presence. He was happy to fly the 7,000 miles from Los Angeles to Windsor Castle to play the most prestigious one-night stand of his life.

Above As godfather to his son Sean (pictured here with mother Yoko Ono), and having directly helped reunite the boy's parents, Elton was deeply affected by John Lennon's violent death in 1980. Taupin would put those feelings into words, penning a heartfelt lyric that Elton would put to music as 'Empty Garden (Hey Hey Johnny)' on the 1982 album 'Jump Up'.

Far right A youthful-looking Elton is pictured in Paris in April 1978 for an appearance on a radio program. A flirtation with contact lenses would prove short-lived, while the longer-lasting collaboration with Taupin would end—temporarily—this month as 'Ego' peaked just inside the UK Top 40.

Right On duty or off, on stage or in the departure lounge, Elton was a paparazzo's dream. The ever-present media spotlight would prove less welcome later in the decade, however, when his marriage got into difficulties and during his bitter court battle with tabloid newspaper *The Sun*.

Center right The addition of another keyboardist left Elton free to emerge from behind the piano when he wished. In the 1990s he would consciously move the keyboard center-stage as the concert grand was replaced by a digital instrument.

Right Andy Gibb and Cliff Richard join Elton on stage. While Andy, younger brother of the Bee Gees, would fall victim to the rock'n'roll lifestyle and die at the criminally early age of 30 and Cliff had no vices whatsoever, Elton steered a middle course—a rock'n'roller who repented.

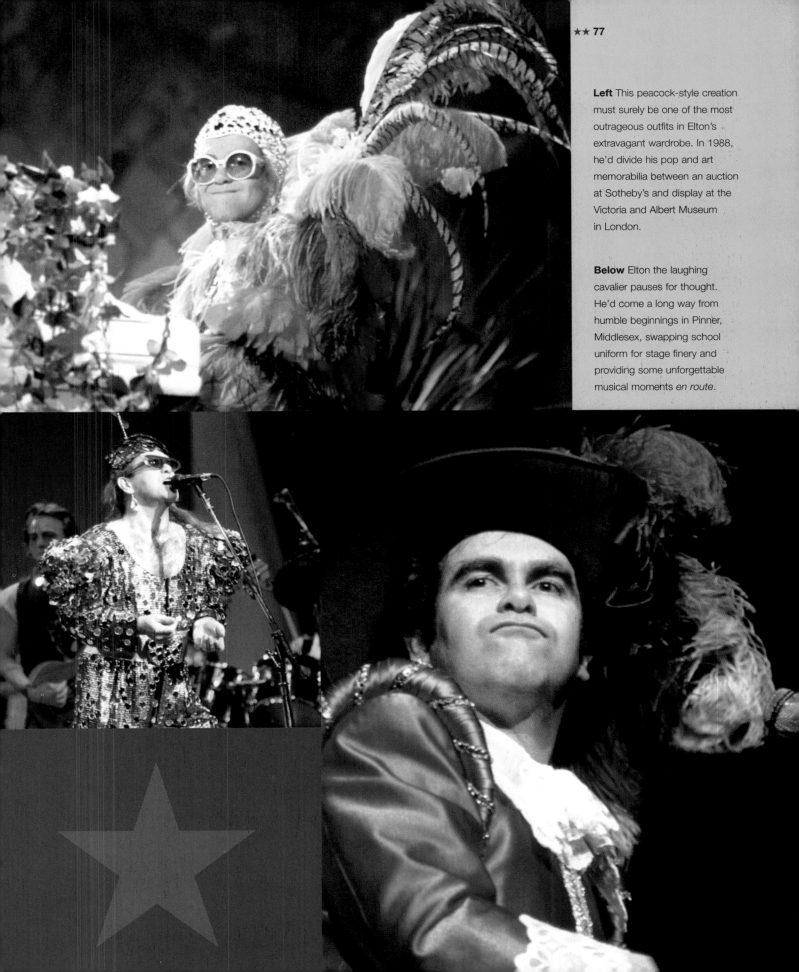

Left This peacock-style creation must surely be one of the most outrageous outfits in Elton's extravagant wardrobe. In 1988, he'd divide his pop and art memorabilia between an auction at Sotheby's and display at the Victoria and Albert Museum in London.

Below Elton the laughing cavalier pauses for thought. He'd come a long way from humble beginnings in Pinner, Middlesex, swapping school uniform for stage finery and providing some unforgettable musical moments *en route*.

Above Elton in 1982 with the recently reassembled 'dream team' of Davey Johnstone, Nigel Olsson and Dee Murray. The next step would be to return to the recording studio in Montserrat for the 'Too Low For Zero' album, the first of the new decade to reach the creative peaks Elton's fans had come to expect during the 1970s.

Opposite Elton in pensive mood. At this stage few knew much about his personal life and relationships. Within a couple of years, even those 'in the know' would be amazed when this confirmed bachelor renounced his status as a single man in favor of matrimony.

It wasn't the first time Elton and Royalty had been linked. As far back as 1972, Princess Margaret had witnessed him playing a charity concert for the National Youth Theatre, and a short while later he'd repeated the favor at the Royal Festival Hall for her Invalid Aid Foundation. Such was the Princess's enthusiasm for Elton's music that an invitation was subsequently extended to play for her mother. That private audience also involved a personalized lyric—"I'd buy Windsor Castle, Your Majesty" replacing the 'big house' line in 'Your Song'.

Prince Andrew's 21st, at which he played to 600 VIP guests while spotlights on the Windsor Castle walls spelled out 'Congratulations', gave him the chance to meet Diana Spencer, the recently betrothed fiancee of Prince Charles.

They were to strike up a real friendship, and one that had plenty of chance to flourish as Elton became involved in raising funds for the Prince's Trust through a series of charity concerts.

Relaxing the Pace

Meanwhile, there was an album to release—yearly now, rather than twice a year. And yet whereas that former punishing schedule had seemed to inspire Elton to ever greater creative heights, one classic album a year now seemed beyond him. 'The Fox' had stalled two places outside the UK Top 10 (reaching Number 21 Stateside), and 'Jump Up', recorded on the Caribbean island of Montserrat again with Chris Thomas at the helm and released in April 1982, performed remarkably similarly, with positions of 13 and

17 respectively. This was surprising, given the advance publicity gained by an excellent new single, 'Blue Eyes' which, at Number 8 in the UK and 12 on the *Billboard* listings was his best performer since 'Song For Guy' in 1978.

The album featured five lyrics from Taupin, four from Gary Osborne (including 'Blue Eyes') and one, 'Legal Boys', from the lyric-writing half of the legendary Tim Rice/Andrew Lloyd Webber partnership that had set the West End ablaze. Their first collaboration was hardly as incendiary as *Jesus Christ Superstar* or *Evita*, but presaged a far more successful second spell in the 1990s. The song selected for first release in the States was the Lennon tribute 'Empty Garden (Hey Hey Johnny)', for which Taupin had supplied the *mots justes*.

Musician-wise, the Who's Pete Townshend weighed in with a guest appearance on 'Ball And Chain' (Chris Thomas had been producing him, hence the connection), but little was being pulled out of the instrumental bag to lift most of the songs out of a frankly unexciting rut.

A Sell-out on Stage

However haphazard his performances on the recording front, Elton's status as a live performer had never been in dispute. And his decision to reunite the original band of Davey, Dee and Nigel for a winter UK tour—his biggest for five years—ensured that tickets sold out in record time. A 14-night stint at London's Hammersmith Odeon took him all the way up to Christmas Eve, and was rapturously received, even though the single 'All Quiet On The Western Front' was buried in a Christmas chart headed by Renée and Renato.

Having turned back the clock by recreating the band from his glory years, and found playing with them was as much fun as ever, the next

logical move was to reunite with Taupin in the hope that the magical combination of words, music, and musicians might kick-start his flagging recording career. And, true to form, it was this dream team that would take him back to the top.

Touring Russia back in 1979, Elton had reassessed his attitude to singing and looked again at the songs he had lived with for so long. Interviewed by *Billboard* in 1997, the 30th year of the John-Taupin relationship, he admitted how surprised he was with what he'd found. "A lot of his lyrics are quite aggressive, and quite down…a lot of dirty little girls and social disease." Now, though, Bernie and his writing partner both had reasons to be cheerful. Following his split with Maxine, Taupin had wed another American, Toni Russo. More interesting still, Elton had been seen with German recording engineer Renate Blauel, who seemed to be playing an important part in his life.

Away from music, Elton's stint as chairman of Watford FC was doing much more than supplying him with a team of willing if untutored backing vocalists. They had been promoted to the First Division, then English football's top flight, in 1982, having risen from the basement division in a mere five years. Interest-free loans running into seven figures from Elton had enabled manager Taylor to play the transfer market and his shrewd acquisitions would ensure that the club was more than prepared to mix it with the best.

The 1982-83 season was to prove a memorable one for Watford and their chairman. Not only would they excel on the field of play, but Elton John would show that he was still a recording artist of some stature.

Above A tour program from 1982, featuring a heartfelt tribute from California-based Bernie Taupin. "He ain't no James Bond," concluded the lyricist, "but nobody does it better." The pair's full-time reunion would shortly prove that point as they produced the first album of exclusively John-Taupin compositions since 1976's 'Blue Moves'.

Above A photo opportunity at Disneyworld. Elton's sense of fun, love of the Disney tradition, and affinity with kids would make him the ideal candidate to write the Oscar-winning soundtrack to 1994's *The Lion King*.

Previous page Elton, wife Renate, and ex-Beatle Ringo Starr enjoy a joke. The two musicians had kept in touch ever since Marc Bolan brought them together in the early 1970s and, having played with John Lennon in 1974, Elton would complete the set by playing with Paul and George in the 1980s under the Prince's Trust banner.

Opposite Any excuse for a spot of cross-dressing! Elton fulfils the role of pantomime dame in December 1984, with charity, as ever, the beneficiary. Earlier in the year he'd been hobnobbing, statesman-like, with Poland's Nobel Prize-winning trade-union leader Lech Walesa, a task he carried off as commendably as this Christmas cracker of a part.

The reunion of Elton and Bernie was good
news for everyone. Everyone, that is, except Dick James, their former music publisher and label boss, for the two now joined forces to issue a writ against him. The seeds of the action had been sown when singer-songwriter Gilbert O'Sullivan—a cloth-capped Elton contemporary of the early 1970s, who'd hit with some disarmingly trite ditties—had successfully sued Gordon Mills who, like Dick James for Elton, had also been his manager, label head, and music publisher. The result was not only the award of back royalties—O'Sullivan also won the copyrights to his songs. It was this 'tables-turning' decision that caused many current superstars to look carefully at their own poorly-paid pasts and consider lawsuits.

It would take until 1985 for the duo's case to get to court, and longer still for it to be decided. Meanwhile, the first musical fruits of the rekindled Elton-Bernie partnership came in June 1983 with 'Too Low For Zero', an album that confirmed the wisdom of their joining forces, combining the immediacy of Elton's recent output with the substance of earlier work. Like the earlier 'Jump Up', it was recorded on Montserrat, the Caribbean island that would be devastated by a volcanic eruption in 1997 but at this time was a popular recording location. The venue was Air Studios, founded by George Martin, and despite the album's downbeat title the sunshine certainly came through in the music.

Album Full of Singles
The first single—'I Guess That's Why They Call It The Blues', released as a taster in late April—was unusual for two reasons: Davey Johnstone joined the pair in the songwriting process for the first (and so far only) time, while the instrumental hook was supplied by Stevie Wonder's harmonica. Motown's former child prodigy had always been a hero, and during the 1973 Yellow Brick Road tour he had been smuggled on board Elton's jetliner as a surprise: the first thing Elton knew was when

Wonder struck up 'Crocodile Rock' from behind the curtained-off rehearsal area!

It wouldn't be the pair's last foray on to recording tape together, and the combination produced Elton's first transatlantic Top 5 single since the Kiki Dee duet. Several other tracks on the album had hit potential: the uptempo 'I'm Still Standing' was the most obvious, making Number 4 in Britain and inspiring a highly imaginative promotional video. MTV was in its infancy, and Elton seized the chance to make an early mark with a song that was nothing less than a personal manifesto.

Two further singles for the album, 'Kiss The Bride' and 'Cold As Christmas', both UK Top 40 entries, made 'Too Low For Zero' the most productive of Elton's albums since 'Yellow Brick Road'. It fared marginally worse than 'Jump Up' in the States where it reached Number 25, but Number 7 at home was the best for six years.

Bizarrely, a dedication on the album, "special thanks to Renarte (sic) Blauel", was to make more headlines than any of the music it contained. The 30-year-old German-born tape operator had in truth played only a small part in the recording, at the overdub and mixing stage back in cold, gray London, but she was clearly to play a larger role in Elton John's life as time went by.

Too Low For Zero

Musicians Elton John (piano, vocals), Davey Johnstone (guitar, vocals), Dee Murray (bass, vocals), Nigel Olsson (drums, vocals), Stevie Wonder *et al*. • **Recorded at** Air Studios, Montserrat • **Top 20 hit singles** 'I Guess That's Why They Call It The Blues' (UK 5, US 4), 'I'm Still Standing' (UK 4, US 12), 'Kiss The Bride' (UK 20, US 25), 'Cold As Christmas' (UK 33) • **Unusual fact** The song 'Kiss The Bride' would be played at confirmed bachelor Elton's wedding a year after this recording • **Track listing** Cold As Christmas • I'm Still Standing • Too Low For Zero • Religion • I Guess That's Why They Call It The Blues • Crystal • Kiss The Bride • Whipping Boy • Saint • One More Arrow • **Commentary** Ten years to the month after 'Yellow Brick Road', Elton came up with his counterpart for the 1980s—not a double, admittedly, but one that re-established not only the songwriting partnership with Bernie but also reassembled the band that had seen most of the 1970s glory days. Strangely, though, the understated cover and the title gave no hint of the excellence of the music • It has been suggested that 'I'm Still Standing' was a message to former US record company Geffen, but it was the video, directed by Russell Mulcahy and with choreography from Arlene Phillips, that matched its arrogance with artistic genius and confirmed Elton as an early MTV favorite. With its brightly colored bodies and sharp editing, it was a landmark clip to go with a landmark album • **Elsewhere in 1983...** Merseyside rock'n'roll legend Billy Fury dies aged 41 of a heart attack • David Bowie starts his Serious Moonlight tour • Irish hard-rockers Thin Lizzy, led by Phil Lynott, call it a day after 13 years • The Clash sack guitarist and co-songwriter Mick Jones • Folk-punk bard Billy Bragg is arrested during anti-apartheid demo in London • 1960s giants the Animals re-form and tour as support to the Police • Diana Ross's free concert in New York's Central Park is rained off • Manchester's Smiths release their first single, 'Hand In Glove' • All the Jam's singles re-chart in the UK in January after their split

Released June 1983

Chart Position UK 7

Chart Position US 25

Producer Chris Thomas

It was an unlikely match, and it took the place of a professional partnership that had been much touted in 1983: a tour with old friend Rod Stewart. The pair had been rehearsing in the summer, testing their combined vocal talents on Motown and soul standards as well as each other's songs. But it never took off, although they'd briefly share a stage in Sun City, and Rod bowed out to record his own 'Camouflage' album on which near-miss Elton guitarist Jeff Beck made a cameo appearance.

Continent-hopping

The year had seen Elton jetsetting even more frantically than usual. When Hollywood played host to the Queen on her historic visit to the United States, he was up there on the top table alongside the Reagans and all manner of expatriate film stars of the Michael Caine class. He'd spent April in North Africa as a guest of the jewelers Cartier's, while the soccer close season found him leading his Watford team round the Great Wall of China—apparently reveling in the fact that this was one of the few places on the globe he wasn't universally recognized and mobbed.

Not that he was entirely out of the public eye. While sightseeing between exhibition matches, Elton doffed his hat at the tomb of Chairman Mao, and unwittingly made headlines worldwide as the press lensmen focused on the fact that an expensive hair transplant, yet officially to be unveiled, seemed to have had little effect.

Unlike his thatch, the love match with Renate continued to flourish. And when the pair marched boldly up the aisle at St. Mark's Church in Darling Point, Sydney, on Valentine's Day 1984 there was no shortage of fans and colleagues wishing the happy couple all the luck

in the world. "She seems the kind of girl who'll keep Elton in his place" concluded proud mum Sheila—but she, like his close circle of friends, must have been surprised at the turn of events. Elton had been that rarity—a rock star with little, if any, sex appeal to trade on.

The relationship had apparently bloomed without anyone in his entourage being aware of what was happening. Quiet meals together had seen love blossom; they had announced their engagement in Australia in early 1984, and though Elton was told he should consider a pre-nuptial agreement to protect his assets should a split later occur he would have none of it. This was clearly romance with a capital R.

The wedding, at which manager John Reid was the best man, was followed by a £100,000 reception at the Sebel Town House hotel. On the other side of the world, however, the *Sunday Mirror* was busily tracking down Linda Woodrow, the first woman to have set her sights on being Mrs Elton John (or, more accurately, Reg Dwight at that time). And when *The Sun*

covered Elton's wedding under the headline "Good On Yer, Poofter"—allegedly a comment from a ribald Australian as the couple emerged from the church—John Reid took exception and cornered the reporter he considered responsible. It was the first of many face-offs the tabloid and Elton John's organization would have in the months to come.

As the new Mrs John, Renate's place was at Elton's side, and she was dutifully present in Wembley Stadium's royal box in May 1984 as he enjoyed his proudest moment yet as Watford's chairman. The occasion was the FA Cup Final against Merseyside giants Everton. And while he shed a tear during the traditional hymn 'Abide With Me', the day was one of delight for the cousin of one-time Wembley warrior Roy Dwight—even if, this time round, the opposition spoiled the happy ending by winning 2-0.

Above Elton, in the guise of Ronald McDonald, embraces Wham! singer George Michael as he bids farewell to teen stardom at Wembley Stadium. Elton hosted a backstage party attended by members of Duran Duran and Frankie Goes To Hollywood, underlining his position as a Godfather of Pop.

Below Music video was in its infancy in the early 1980s, and it was clear a showman like Elton could use it as a springboard to relaunch his career. This he proceeded to do with a series of vibrant clips to illustrate such songs as 'Passengers' and 'I'm Still Standing'.

Renate was also with Elton on his next recording date, engineering the sessions for the June release of 'Breaking Hearts'. Again recorded in the Montserrat sun, the album gave Elton back-to-back UK Top 10 singles in 'Sad Songs (Say So Much)' and 'Passengers'. This helped boost it to a Number 2 placing behind the late Bob Marley's 'Legend' hit collection—Elton's highest album in Britain since the heady days of 'Caribou'. In the States, 'Sad Songs' was his best-performing single since 1980, all of which indicated that the reunion of the 'dream team' had yet to run out of steam.

'Passengers' was Bernie's comment on apartheid—which was ironic since, in February of that year, anti-apartheid demonstrators had protested outside Elton's hotel in New Zealand at his decision to play the South African holiday resort of Sun City with Rod Stewart in 1983. Other album highlights included 'In Neon' (a US-only single, while Britain got the title track), 'Who Wears These Shoes' (another Stateside success) and 'Slow Down Georgie'.

Music to Change the World

If Elton had served his musical apprenticeship in the 1960s, an era when music, it seemed, really could change the world, 1985 was the year in which it finally made a difference. The catalyst was, of course, Live Aid—and Elton was there, along with fellow 1960s survivors the Who, Stones, and Status Quo, to play a part in a unique day.

Most acts were restricted to four songs, but Elton, ever the master showman, somehow managed to squeeze in five. Perhaps it was because he shared the spotlight on two occasions—the inevitable 'Don't Go Breaking My Heart' with the ever-faithful Kiki Dee in attendance and 'Don't Let The Sun Go Down On Me' with current pop idol George Michael, of whom much more later. His set list was completed by 'I'm Still Standing', the US chart-topping 'Bennie And The Jets', and 'Rocket Man', all performed in a velvet smoking jacket despite the heat. Live Aid organizer Bob Geldof explained that the piano man had been one of the first names on his list of invitations. "His music obviously speaks for itself, but personally he is one of the kindest people I have ever met and certainly one of the bravest."

Elton graced Wembley Stadium's stage once again two weeks later, adding his blessing to the career of George Michael, a 22-year-old singer-songwriter he felt could already be mentioned in the same breath as Paul McCartney. George was a north London boy like himself, who'd served his time as a teen heartthrob with Wham! and was now dissolving his partnership with guitarist Andrew Ridgeley to go solo in a more serious vein. The pair hammed it up, with Elton in full disguise, and George sang 'Candle In The Wind' to Elton's piano accompaniment to provide the event's most moving moment.

"Live Aid organizer Bob Geldof explained that the piano man had been one of the first names on his list of invitations"

An All-star Album

Back in March, a pearl-festooned Elton had been on stage at the Ivor Novello awards, perhaps the most prestigious forum for honoring songwriters through past decades of pop (and one that had recognized him on several occasions), to present George with the Songwriter of the Year accolade. The younger man had already reciprocated at Live Aid, and the double act would reconvene once more on Elton's next album, 'Ice On Fire', sessions for which would begin shortly.

Having gradually reassembled his backing band and reunited with his songwriting partner, the new album would see the return of Gus Dudgeon to replace Chris Thomas, initially at the suggestion of manager John Reid. A lot of water had flowed under the bridge since he'd left Rocket under a cloud, but he must have been flattered to be given total control of everything, right down to the hiring of the musicians for the sessions (Dee and Nigel having left the fold for a second time after 'Breaking Hearts'). Thus it was that a core band of Davey Johnstone, Fred Mandel (keyboards), David Paton (bass, ex-Pilot), and Dave Mattacks (drums, from folk-rockers Fairport Convention) were augmented by a selection of all-star guests: Queen's rhythm section of John Deacon and Roger Taylor, and Nik Kershaw, with US soul sirens Sister Sledge contributing backing vocals to the opening 'This Town'.

Above Elton is congratulated by promoter Harvey Goldsmith on the stage of Live Aid, as organizer Bob Geldof looks on. "It is an outstanding achievement and it will be the concert of the decade," he told BBC news in the run-up to the event, which the master showman graced with a five-song set.

Right Film director Ken Russell, who'd worked with Elton on *Tommy*, renewed the association a decade later with the video for 1985's 'Nikita'. The concept of Western man falling for Communist girl led to scenes like this one. The song, with echoes of 'Daniel', would be his most successful single for some time.

Right Elton clutches an award for record concert ticket sales in the States. His stature as a live draw on both sides of the Atlantic was rarely in doubt through his career, and the need to entertain on stage remains a motivating force for Elton in the 1990s.

Far Right Another scene from the 'Nikita' video which included a somewhat unlikely dream sequence at Watford's Vicarage Road ground. The Pinball Wizard boots, retained from *Tommy*, gave him an unfair advantage over other fans.

Right Having been the presenter in 1985 when George Michael was honored, 1986 saw Elton on the receiving end at the Ivors when he and Bernie were rewarded for their Outstanding Services to British Music, as well as the Best Song for 'Nikita'. He interrupted a European tour in April to attend.

Left Elton picks up an award in 1986 for Dutch sales of 'Nikita'. Elton's ability to write a chart-topper was still in question until 'Sacrifice', a similarly-paced ballad, emerged at the end of the decade. 'The Man Who Never Died', the instrumental B-side of 'Nikita', was a bonus track unavailable elsewhere.

Above Elton identified very strongly with Prince Charles' work with young people undertaken through the Prince's Trust, and would regularly appear at its charity rock gigs with other members of the music-business hierarchy. Said Elton, "The Prince and his lovely young wife have captured the imagination of the young people of England." The only drawback: "Charles, unlike Diana, doesn't like rock'n'roll."

Left Elton's live performances have always included a highly theatrical element. Here he makes a late 1984 charity appearance with that giant of the British theater, Sir John Gielgud.

"Elton and Bernie would be considerably richer as a result of Judge Nicholls' decision"

Above Elton and Renate attended the wedding of the Duke and Duchess of York on 23 July 1986. Both bride and groom were big fans (Andrew having had him entertain at his 21st), and Elton re-recorded his hit 'Song For Guy', Fergie's favorite song, in a solo piano version as a wedding present.

George Michael played a leading role on two tracks, contributing backing vocals to 'Nikita' and a featured harmony vocal on 'Wrap Her Up': whether or not Elton wrote it with his duet partner in mind, the latter bore the Wham! trademark, and both would be released as singles. 'Nikita' inspired an interesting video that reunited Elton and director Ken Russell for the first time since *Tommy* to create a tale of forbidden love across the Berlin Wall, but it wasn't a song that would work well in concert. Even so, its musical echoes of 'Daniel' took it to the transatlantic Top 10, making it one of his biggest singles in years. If he continued to rely on the tried and tested, it seemed, he would do well.

Talking of traditions, the pre-Christmas residency, always over-subscribed, had by now transferred to the 7,000-seat Wembley Arena, and every one of this year's nine nights was sold out. BBC Radio 1 broadcast live to the ticketless

masses on the 15th, while Rod Stewart and George Michael popped in to make the final night particularly memorable.

The next single release had nothing at all to do with the 'Ice On Fire' album. This four-person effort was to prove both a one-off and the first in a long-running saga. Elton shared billing with Dionne Warwick, Stevie Wonder, and Gladys Knight on 'That's What Friends Are For', a song from the pen of master tunesmith Burt Bacharach intended to raise funds for AIDS research. The song would be the first new Number 1 of 1986 in the States, reaching the Top 20 back home, and the feeling of making a difference in fighting the killer disease was clearly one he appreciated. The 1990s would see the Elton John Aids Foundation formed, with all his singles royalties dedicated to finding a cure.

Talking of royalties, the court saga with Dick James that had been rumbling on since 1983 was finally settled after three years when, on 29 January 1986, Judge Nicholls' decision was handed down. Elton John and Bernie Taupin would be considerably richer as a result, by an undisclosed sum variously described as between one and five million pounds. Unlike Gilbert O'Sullivan, however, they were unable to reclaim their song copyrights or ownership of the original recordings.

The judgment concluded that DJM's foreign subsidiaries had been creaming off too much from Elton and Bernie's writing royalties—a considerable matter for an act with world-wide sales in their millions, and a fact of which they, in their naiveté, seemed to be unaware. The original 1967 publishing agreement, too, was considered an "unfair transaction", while the 1968 recording contract, though improved in 1970, was also damned.

The money the pair were to be paid redressed all three of those wrongs. But given that DJM had given Elton his leg-up to fame, that he had profited from their hard work on his behalf, that Dick James and Elton had got on well (a father and son-type relationship, according to James) and that considerable time had passed, damages were all that would be awarded. Elton could not reclaim his 'babies'. Dick James' health, already failing, seemed to go downhill after the judgment and in early February he died of a massive heart attack. A compassionate Elton agreed to pay James' legal costs as a goodwill gesture.

Sharing the Limelight

Instead of arguing about royalty rates, the summer of 1986 saw Elton and Renate hobnobbing with real-life Royalty once again. Having entertained Prince Andrew on his 21st, the piano man was guaranteed a seat along with his wife in Westminster Abbey when Sarah Ferguson became the Duchess of York, while a few weeks earlier he'd been happy to appear in a rock concert to be staged in aid of the Prince's Trust.

The spirit of Live Aid would clearly be continued under that umbrella—with support, it appeared, from Princess Diana—and the bill of Eric Clapton, Tina Turner, Phil Collins, and Paul McCartney, to name just a big-name quartet, showed that the rock aristocracy was more than happy to collaborate. Elton weighed in with a typically impassioned 'I'm Still Standing' to take the Trust, celebrating its tenth anniversary, into the rock age.

Sharing the limelight, as he gladly did on this occasion, was clearly something that came easily to Elton John, and he decided to indulge in some duet activity. Having started with George

Michael, he further showed his versatility by teaming up in quick succession with Millie Jackson, Cliff Richard, and Jennifer Rush. 'Act Of War', his duet with daring soul songstress Jackson, came about when Tina Turner rejected the song, and it had actually been the first single to be peeled off 'Ice On Fire'. The pair had performed it together at the Montreux Festival to rapturous applause, and the fact it failed to make the Top 30 suggests it might have been better remaining a live item.

'Slow Rivers', with Cliff Richard, was one of three duets the former Rocket (US) recording artist was to release in 1986. The others were 'Living Doll' with comedy team the Young Ones, and 'All I Ask Of You' from *Phantom Of The Opera* which teamed him with Sarah Brightman. Both of these enjoyed better chart fortunes, despite Elton and Cliff performing their Number 44 collaboration in a November TV special *Cliff From The Hip*. The song reappeared on the next album 'Leather Jackets', although 'Flames Of Paradise', a later release performed with the statuesque Jennifer Rush, proved even harder to find once the single had fallen from a disappointing Number 59 peak.

"The summer of 1986 saw Elton and Renate hobnobbing with real-life Royalty once again"

Below The pairing of Elton with American soul star Millie Jackson, famed for her outspoken mid-song rap, might have been expected to produce fireworks. 'Act Of War' was only a Number 32 UK hit, however, and the partnership was not one rekindled on 1993's 'Duets' collection.

'Leather Jackets' appeared in November 1986 but, despite perfect timing for the pre-Christmas market, it only reached Number 24 in Britain and a surprising Number 91 Stateside. It introduced an unfamiliar recording venue in the Wisseloord Studio, Hilversum, Holland. Gary Osborne reappeared as lyricist for just one song, 'Memory Of Love' (probably an old one Elton had stockpiled), while Cher contributed a lyric to 'Don't Trust That Woman'.

The Queen duo of Deacon and Taylor made a one-track contribution for the second album running, on 'Angeline', for which Elton and Bernie were joined as writers by backing vocalist Alan Carvell. Producer Dudgeon thanked the musicians on his sleeve note for "good times, long hours, and hard work", but there seemed a rather larger percentage of perspiration than inspiration on this album.

It had not been a memorable year—even being presented with a belated Brit award for his Russian tour of 1979 by Conservative politician Norman Tebbit had resulted in a tantrum. Better had come at the Ivors, when 'Nikita' was voted Best Song, and Elton's

Outstanding Contribution to British Music was noted and honored. A sunshine pick-me up was needed, and Australia—always a loyal market for Elton, especially after he'd reciprocated by getting married there—was the chosen venue. A 27-date tour was penned in for the last two months of 1986, for which Elton packed some very special outfits, wigs, and props.

A Mouth-watering Prospect

Things were going so well that arrangements were made to capture one of the concerts live, the Melbourne Symphony Orchestra being recruited to add string arrangements to the ballads under the baton of former band member James Newton Howard. The prospect was a mouth-watering one; after all, the only live efforts up until now had been a radio broadcast and 'Here And There', an effort that had seen the light of day only thanks to the DJM contract. This would be the real thing, showing Elton in his element—and to up the stakes further, an estimated ten million TV viewers would be watching!

Audiences had already seen him play two sets—a 'popular' selection, with Elton prancing in Mohican wig and Tina Turner miniskirt (not at the same time!) in front of a 13-piece band, and a 'classical' selection backed by the 88-piece orchestra. For the latter, he dressed as Mozart, with a frock coat and beauty spot—but all this showmanship couldn't disguise the fact that his voice was shot. On 9 December he collapsed on stage, causing great concern, and, with the day of the telecast approaching, there was clearly a problem with his throat. The doctors' advice was to stop performing straight away, pending further tests. And should the nodules on his vocal chords prove to be less than benign, the silence could be permanent…

"...but all this showmanship couldn't disguise the fact that his voice was shot"

Below Noel Edmonds chats with Elton at the 1986 Brit Awards—a ceremony he later denounced as "a load of rubbish." Part of the problem may have been that he was picking up an Outstanding Achievement prize for his Russian tour seven years before, or that the presenter was hard-line Tory Norman Tebbit.

Left Elton struts the stage Down Under in Tina Turner guise. Behind the painted smile was a considerably worried man, for there seemed a real chance at one stage that the problem nodules on his vocal chords could be cancerous. The operation to remove them would mean this was the last the world heard from him in a musical sense for some considerable time.

The year of 1987 should have been one of reflection as Elton reached 40, the ripe old age at which life is reputed to begin. He should by now have had no doubts about his own longevity or his musical worth, having proved all there was to prove and clocked up a hat-trick of Top 10 albums in the recent past. Sadly, despite an optimistic start when his throat was given the all clear after benign nodules had been lasered away, it was to be a year that was remembered for a good deal more than a milestone birthday.

Previous page Elton wigs out in typical style. The next four years would prove his most hair-raising to date.

Opposite Elton and Bernie celebrated the 20th anniversary of their writing partnership in 1987. Success had changed their lifestyles immeasurably— substitute Windsor for Pinner, Los Angeles for Lincolnshire— but the mix of words and music was still capable of producing results.

Below right A pair of the famous stackheels that had become Elton's trademark in the early 1970s went under the auctioneer's hammer at Sotheby's as Elton divested himself of two decades' worth of stage clothes and memorabilia.

The Johns' marriage had long been the subject of speculation and, after three years, appeared to be over in March when a formal split was announced. In the event, it would merely be a brief, month-long parting, but one that inevitably re-established the pair as a gossip-column staple.

The change in Renate over the years of their marriage had been marked, externally at any rate, her former jeans and sweatshirt wardrobe being replaced by designer outfits that enhanced her dark good looks to perfection. Yet the good life seemed to have been gained at a price: Philip Norman's 1991 book *Elton*, the nearest thing to an authorized biography published to date, analyzes the couple's relationship in great detail. He paints a picture of a woman who, having given up her independence and her flat in Kilburn, was living in someone else's house, surrounded by many years of accumulated possessions, while her partner—its owner—pursued both his career and, Norman hints, the homosexual side of his lifestyle he had hoped that marriage might suppress.

There was a sad echo of the Dwights' home life in the fact that, just as his father had been absent serving King

and country, touring had kept Elton away from Woodside for so many months of each year. Despite an avowed intention to continue her own career as an engineer and, latterly, record producer, Renate was left to live what seems to have been (excluding a live-in housekeeper and handyman) a solitary existence.

It's been suggested that one of Elton's reasons for getting married was his mother's wish to become a grandparent; jokingly or otherwise, her wedding gift to the pair had been a baby buggy. Yet this would remain gathering dust alongside Elton's many other possessions—and it was probably no coincidence that, when he and Renate finally split, he would dramatically divest himself of two full decades' worth of memorabilia, furnishings and *objets d'art* in an apparent attempt to draw a line under his life and start again from scratch…a single man and a simpler man.

The press had highlighted the fact that Renate had not been at Elton's side in Australia, an implicit accusation of indifference she understandably refuted in a rare interview with the *Daily Express*. She revealed that daily contact had been maintained by phone to both parties' satisfaction: "I had been told by the doctors that it was not serious. Elton had said there was no need for me to be there." The *Sunday People* told a different story, claiming he asked her to come but she declined. Yet another twist was added when Renate's

relationship with ex-Kissing the Pink singer Sylvia Griffin—whom she was producing, and for whom Elton and Gary Osborne had apparently written a song—was suggested to have "hidden depths."

It was good news that she'd returned for, in the light of events this year, Elton was in need of someone to stand alongside him. *The Sun*, the newspaper with the largest British daily sale, had targeted him with a series of allegations regarding his private life that would take him back to court so soon after the Dick James case. This time it was his reputation, not royalties and copyrights, that was at stake. *The Sun* had splashed the first sex and drugs allegations across

its pages in February, continuing with the stories even after legal action had commenced. *The Daily Mirror*, the other leading tabloid, then rallied to Elton's defense. And while they clearly had their own agenda in denouncing their rival's stories as false, their claim that Elton had been in New York on the day *The Sun*'s 'reliable witness' had said he was busy indulging in an orgy at a house in Berkshire clearly cast doubt on the truth of the 'exclusives'.

Back in Britain

Having canceled all concerts for the year, Elton decided to return from Australia in March "for my wife, my future and my fans. I'm coming home to clear my name". He was thus in Britain to celebrate his 40th birthday, though in view of the circumstances it was a defiant rather than a carefree affair at John Reid's Rickmansworth home. Guests included the Yorks, Eric Clapton, Phil Collins, and Beatles George and Ringo.

In April, he briefly broke his public silence to appear at an AIDS benefit show in London—a very rare appearance in what was to prove the quietest year of his musical life. "I plan to give my voice a sabbatical, at least a year and a bit, to get my momentum back", he said—and had suited actions to words while in Australia by playing piano as guest of Lionel Richie but declining to sing. Musically speaking, then, 1987 would prove a tale of two records. 'Greatest Hits Volume 3' had been a compilation spanning 1979-87 to conclude his spell with Geffen—but if the label had anticipated a repeat of its predecessors' Number 1 and Number 21 chart positions it would be sorely disappointed with a Number 84 showing. Elton's future releases would be on his former US label MCA, starting with 'Live In Australia'.

Below Manager John Reid leads Elton away from the court after crossing swords with *The Sun*. The tabloid, owned by Australian magnate Rupert Murdoch, made two major public relations mistakes in the 1980s—attempting to crucify Elton and blackening the reputation of the Liverpool fans involved in 1989's Hillsborough disaster. Both would lose it readers.

"Few suspected 'Candle In The Wind' would go higher still one decade later, albeit in tragic circumstances"

The album's choices had certainly been blasts from the past: all but three dated from his DJM period, and even these 'newies' dated from 1974 ('Don't Let The Sun…') and 1976 ('Sorry Seems To Be…' and the underrated 'Tonight'). Elton admitted he'd even had to relearn the words to some of the songs, six of which had originally appeared on his eponymous breakthrough album—but emphasized how that process had made him appreciate afresh the genius of his wordsmith.

That Elton's Australian concert souvenir had been of such a high quality was a tribute both to the singer and long-serving producer Gus Dudgeon. His voice had been in such a delicate state coming into the shows that audience members had suspected a problem with the microphones—the singer's mouth would keep on opening and closing, but momentary gaps in the sound betrayed to the watching Dudgeon that all was not well. Apparently Elton had been ready to cancel the final performance, the one due to be televised, but summoned up his courage and went on to give all he had.

Miraculously, the majority of the album selections (other nights also having been recorded) were from this climactic finale—a tribute to Elton's professionalism and never-say-die spirit.

In Britain, the live album was presented as a box set containing two vinyl disks and it did relatively poorly, crawling to a paltry Number 70 (24 in the States was very much more respectable), but the second single extracted from it, 'Candle In The Wind' found greater favor. By reaching Number 5 (UK) and 6 (US), it far outshone its studio predecessor, though few suspected it would go higher still one decade later, albeit in tragic circumstances.

Cowboy in the States

Bernie had meanwhile been living a quiet life with new wife Toni, ironically in the same house he'd bought in Los Angeles back in 1972. Having flown his parents out to join him, he'd become an American citizen—and his adopted country rewarded him with two chart-topping singles. 'We Built This City' (Starship) and 'These Dreams' (Heart) were written with a fellow expatriate, musician Martin Page, while he'd also released the third in a series of low-key solo albums.

Elton's position at Watford FC was beyond question: despite the public mudslinging, he still embodied everything the club held dear. But the departure of Graham Taylor for Aston Villa

Left Many people may have been unaware of Elton's talent on the acoustic guitar, but judging by Davey Johnstone's expression, the novelty had long since worn off—or maybe he just wasn't hitting the right note!

Below Elton takes a bow with Lionel Richie. The pair shared a stage in Australia, but Elton was under strict instructions not to strain his vocal chords and contented himself with piano accompaniment, writing anything he wanted to say on a small chalk board he carried with him.

"After *The Sun* resumed its offensive in April, he decided to take the bull by the horns and appear on TV to refute the rumors."

Above Elton, the Beach Boys, and sundry other music legends at the Rock'n'Roll Hall of Fame. The annual induction ceremonies were often an excuse for an all-star jam session. Elton inducted the Beach Boys in January 1988, and six years later was happy to enter the ranks of rock's all-time greats himself, courtesy of Axl Rose.

at the end of the 1986-87 season after exactly a decade at the helm would weaken the bond between the club and its chairman, and as early as April of 1987 newspapers were suggesting his reign might also be reaching an end. Elton—who had graciously demanded no compensation from Villa, happy for Taylor to better himself—was at pains to insist that, now he'd stopped touring, the turnover needed to sustain his investment simply wasn't there.

He was equally adamant, however, that while negotiations were under way to sell his stake, this would only be to someone with the club's interests very much at heart and the financial muscle to deliver on their promises. It would emerge in November that newspaper magnate Robert Maxwell was the chosen one, his suitability underlined by the fact that his BPCC printing operation was locally based. But the Football League stepped in to block the deal since Maxwell already owned Derby County and his son was chairman of Oxford United. Even though an employee had been nominated as chairman, this was clearly a step too far.

In retrospect, it was a narrow escape for Watford given Maxwell's posthumous unmasking as a somewhat unscrupulous businessman. By the following year, Elton had re-pledged himself to the cause, planning to invest a further £500,000 in an attempt to get the club back to the top-flight status it had enjoyed under Taylor and lost in the season following his departure. Back in 1987, though, clearing the Elton John name was the main event, and after *The Sun* resumed its offensive in April, he decided to take the bull by the horns and appear on Michael Parkinson's TV show to refute the rumors.

The pair were old friends, and it could hardly be said that Elton was given a rough ride—yet it's fair to say that this slice of prime-time television took the initiative away from the tabloid. In its turn, *The Sun* had claimed to have a photo of Elton "too disgusting to print in a family newspaper" and smugly advised its readers that "If you believe Elton, you'll believe in fairies." The allegations and lawsuits would rumble on until the year's end.

A Better New Year

After the depressing days of 1987, Elton started the new year in optimistic fashion by inducting old friends and influences the Beach Boys into the US Rock'n'Roll Hall of Fame. In the light of the recent single success of the live 'Candle In The Wind', and with no new album yet in the can, Rocket repromoted 'Live In Australia' without its original deluxe packaging and were rewarded when it advanced to a more respectable Number 43 in Britain.

That his marriage seemed alive and well seemed confirmed in March 1988 when Mr and Mrs John were seen canoodling at Renate's lavish 35th birthday party at Brown's restaurant in London's Covent Garden. Yet Elton could well have done with her calmly efficient help in the studio, a newspaper report suggesting that a number of new recordings had been accidentally erased from the master tape. Looking on the bright side, it was good to know that his singing voice had emerged unscathed from the laser surgery and the enforced period of silence that had followed.

His voice had gone down in pitch, he reported, before revealing with understandable delight that he'd got his falsetto back—clearly a matter of some concern. Gus Dudgeon, who had proved to be a miracle worker in Australia, had unexpectedly been replaced by Chris Thomas in a game of producers' musical chairs, and the 'newcomer' recruited some even more familiar faces in a star-studded backing choir. The Beach Boys, Dee Murray, and Nigel Olsson were among those lending their voices to an album that would see the former Reg Dwight pay an unexpected return visit to the name he'd left behind with such relief at the beginning of the 1970s.

A stage return was next on the agenda, and it came in June at London's Royal Albert Hall where he dipped a toe into familiar waters as part of the Prince's Trust Gala. Over £2 million was raised, thanks to a bill that included young Stock-Aitken-Waterman pop protégé Rick Astley and old stagers Joe Cocker and Leonard Cohen among usual suspects Collins, Clapton, Midge Ure, and the Bee Gees. The following month would see the release of the new album,

'Reg Strikes Back': its cover showed him surrounded by various pieces of memorabilia—over 2,000 of his personal effects were to go under the hammer at Sotheby's on 8 September—and this, combined with the title, seemed to indicate a new chapter in his life. Sadly, it was to go on without Renate: news of the final split came on 17 November.

Though understandably dispirited—"I feel this terrible guilt; she was so supportive when things were going badly for me"—the album's success must have been a boost to morale. A US Number 2 placing for the lead-off single 'I Don't Want To Go On With You Like That', was his best solo showing for a decade, and the album made it into both British and American Top 20s at 18 and 16 respectively. In deference to the current dance culture, one-time Madonna producer Shep Pettibone was permitted to do a 12-inch mix of the single, but long-time fans would be relieved to learn that Elton

Above left A public show of affection at Renate's birthday party in March was not to prove the good omen it seemed. Eight months later, the couple's separation was confirmed. Elton was a single man again.

Below The video medium continued to be kind to Elton, and he was to confirm his relevance with clips like this one, filmed to accompany the November 1988 release of the single 'A Word In Spanish'.

Right Despite having graced more awards ceremonies than most, Elton was still happy to pick up the accolades—in this case from the American Society of Composers, Authors and Publishers, in company with Mark Knopfler, Billy Ocean, and Boy George.

Center and below right The scene at Sotheby's auction rooms as the mementos of Elton's past life are prepared to be sold to the highest bidder. The jacket on the left-hand mannequin can be seen being worn by Elton on page 99. The Pinball Wizard boots fetched £11,000! Other items to reach high prices included a photo of Elvis, signed "To Elton" (£2,500), and the Eiffel Tower hat pictures opposite (£3,800).

Right Despite his personal problems, Elton continued to keep his customary high profile. This eye-catching suit suggested an affinity with his fans north of the border— but as to which tartan he was wearing he remained tight-lipped.

Left Elton and Renate in Paris, the city of lovers. Elton's headgear indicates he is fairly certain of his whereabouts—or has he gone temporarily in-Seine?

Below left Yet more problems with hats as he adopts the look that would forever be associated with his 1990 chart-topper 'Sacrifice'. The significance of the crucifix is uncertain, but the venue is a book launch by noted LA photographer Herb Ritts.

Bottom left The Eiffel Tower gives way to the Chrysler Building as Elton and John Reid celebrate in true Stateside style. Reid left his job running the UK arm of Motown Records in 1971 to manage Elton and has been there ever since, despite the occasional 'outside' client like Queen.

Below A sight for sore eyes… This selection of spectacles from Elton's collection was among the lots on view at Sotheby's. His illuminated 'Elton' specs sold for £9,000, while others sold for between £2,000-£3,200.

(or was it Reg?) had not 'gone disco' this time round. Taupin had weighed in with a clutch of above-average lyrics, but with the troubles that had been afflicting his partner's non-musical life, a classic Elton album would perhaps have been expecting too much.

It would be the solidly traditional 'A Word In Spanish', a track that might have come off 'Blue Moves', that would give him a successful US follow-up single. Elsewhere, the opening chugger, 'Town Of Plenty', featured the Who's Pete Townshend guesting on guitar, while the early Hercules period was recalled by 'Mona Lisas And Mad Hatters Part 2', the title alluding to one of the standout tracks on 1972's 'Honky Chateau'. Despite the previously named backing vocal guests (the Beach Boys making their presence felt on 'Since God Created Girls'), the core band was the now-familiar one of Davey Johnstone (guitar), David Paton (bass), Charlie Morgan (drums), and Fred Mandel (additional keyboards), with Ray Cooper dropping in to add his percussive talents to a handful of selections.

With American adulation once again exceeding his status at home (where the newspaper-reading public could have been forgiven for having had their fill of Elton John, through no fault of his own), Elton decided to kick off a world tour at New York Madison Square Garden. It had always been a favorite venue, especially given the John Lennon connection, and five consecutive dates took the house record from American music legends Grateful Dead. Support act was Wet Wet Wet, a Scottish white-soul quartet who would go on to bigger things. Elton had made a habit of talent

Above The catalogue produced for the auction of Elton's memorabilia itself became a collector's item.

Below This spangled baseball-style cap was sold at the first of Elton's fund-raising 'Out Of The Closet' charity shop sales.

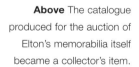

spotting, yet even he could see the funny side when 'I Don't Want To Go On With You Like That' just failed to give him his first *Billboard* solo chart-topper since 'Island Girl'. For sitting there, immovable, at the summit was none other than…George Michael!

Vindicated at Last

Elton and Renate had gone their separate ways in 1988, but the year would end on a happier note in December when his legal battle with *The Sun* was resolved to his satisfaction. The tabloid's many and various accusations had been proved unfounded, not least because their chief witness turned his coat and chose the *Daily Mirror* as the medium through which to admit his lies. Meanwhile, a report that Elton had removed the vocal chords of guard dogs he owned was to prove the final straw: faced with this latest, demonstrably false story, *The Sun* capitulated totally and led their 12 December front page with a 'Sorry Elton' headline, combining this with an out of court settlement estimated at £1 million.

"We are delighted," smarmed the tabloid, "that Elton and *The Sun* have become friends again, and are very sorry that we were lied to by a teenager living in a world of fantasy." Happily his fans had never believed the innuendo, and the paper had reportedly found its sales decreasing each time a new fabrication appeared.

Honor satisfied, the way was clear for Elton to resume his musical career with a vengeance. The coming year of 1989 saw him break with tradition and play a compact digital keyboard on stage rather than his customary grand piano. Far more importantly than that, he came up with an album that celebrated his musical roots and brought him his first ever solo UK

"Honor satisfied, the way was clear for Elton to resume his musical career with a vengeance"

Left Elton traded his trademark grand piano for a smaller digital keyboard in 1989. This enabled him to command center stage, rather than viewing his audience sideways, and gave the stage set a more satisfactory, symmetrical appearance.

Above Always happy to show support for pop's younger generation, he swaps notes with keyboardist Adam Tinley, better known as Adamski, whose 'Killer' topped the UK singles charts in 1990.

Sleeping With The Past

Musicians Elton John (piano, vocals), Davey Johnstone (guitar, vocals), et al. • **Recorded at** Puk Studios, Denmark • **Top 20 hit singles** 'Healing Hands' (UK 45, US 13), 'Sacrifice' (US 18), 'Sacrifice'/'Healing Hands' (reissue) (UK 1), 'Club At The End Of the Street' (UK 47, US 28) • **Unusual fact** Bernie was an unusual presence at the recording sessions, a fact that led Elton to dedicate the resulting album to him • **Track listing** Durban Deep • Healing Hands • Whispers • Club At The End Of The Street • Sleeping With The Past • Stone's Throw From Hurtin' • Sacrifice • I Never Knew Her Name • Amazes Me • Blue Avenue • **Commentary** Reviews of this album were all but written before it appeared: Q, for instance, thought it "won't do much to change the fact that he's better known for his football team, his court cases and his souvenirs than for his music." It would take nine months, but the chart-topping performance of 'Sleeping With The Past' must have been accompanied by the sound of words being eaten • "The first thing I've done for years without personal problems clouding my mind" was Elton's own assessment, and the album's joyously retro feel took one back to another Number 1, 1973's 'Don't Shoot Me...'. Regardless of 'Sacrifice's delayed-reaction performance, this would have been a landmark in its own right in an era of frankly ordinary Elton albums • **Elsewhere in 1989...** 1960s singer Gene Pitney returns to the top of the UK charts with Marc Almond and 'Something's Gotten Hold Of My Heart' • Former Janet Jackson choreographer Paula Abdul becomes a hit US recording star • Band Aid II cover 'Do They Know It's Christmas' to chart-topping effect • Jive Bunny and the Mastermixers are this year's UK chart sensation • Milli Vanilli top the US chart, but would later be revealed as models who didn't actually sing on their records • The re-formed Who sell 46,000 tickets for a New York 25th anniversary concert • Axl Rose, lead singer with Guns 'N' Roses, announces their disbandment (later rescinded) due to members' drug problems

Released September 1989

Chart Position UK 1 (5weeks)

Chart Position US 23

Producer Chris Thomas

Number 1 single. The album was 'Sleeping With The Past', and the intention had been to create a 'Captain Fantastic'-style concept piece that cast an affectionate glance over the shoulder to the early-1960s days when black music reigned supreme and Bluesology backed its brightest stars. This 'musical tribute' approach was a tactic his friend Billy Joel had used successfully six years earlier with 'An Innocent Man'—and, having proven his own innocence concerning *The Sun*'s baseless slurs, Elton was on a roll.

The speed of the compositional process was frightening, the title track apparently taking little over two hours from sight of the lyric for the music to fall into place and a basic recording to be laid down. Other highlights of an album Elton would dedicate to his lyricist were the Drifters-influenced 'Club At The End Of The Street' (also extracted as a single) and the gospelly 'I Never Knew Her Name'.

Topping the UK Charts

The album, Elton's first to be recorded in Denmark, reached Number 6 first time out— a respectable enough showing, indeed his best since 'Ice On Fire'. Yet the success of 'Sacrifice' (reissued as a double A-side with 'Healing Hands' and giving Elton his first solo UK Number 1 after regular plays from Radio 1 DJ Steve Wright) reinvigorated the long-player and ensured it became his first album chart-topper at home since 'Caribou'. (Surprisingly, US fans only afforded it Number 23 status.) It was followed in October 1990 with a double 'Very Best Of', the first compilation to be designed specifically for compact disk, which predictably cleaned up sales-wise and topped the UK charts for five summer weeks.

"Elton collapsed on stage during a dance routine, but recovered sufficiently to celebrate his 42nd birthday in typically lavish style."

The world-wide jaunt that followed the release of 'Sleeping', with one-time guitarist Nik Kershaw playing support, was eventful even by Elton's standards—while in Paris, he actually collapsed on stage during a dance routine, but recovered sufficiently to celebrate his 42nd birthday in typically lavish style. Six nights at Wembley climaxed the UK tour leg, a duet with soul diva Aretha Franklin, 'Through The Storm', riding high in the charts as he did so. Then, in August, he guested in an all-star American-staged performance of the Who's *Tommy*, reprising his time-honored Pinball Wizard role at London's Royal Albert Hall in November.

After a run of several highly eventful years, 1990 was expected to be thankfully low-key for Elton John. His problems had taken a dreadful personal toll, and he was persuaded to take time off from his recording and touring schedule to spend six weeks in a Chicago clinic getting over problems with drink, drugs, and the slimming disease bulimia. He'd just relocated to Atlanta because of a relationship, and he grew to love it there "because it wasn't Los Angeles or New York." This would be the home of a new, cleaned-up Elton John—a place where he could enjoy normality, "be free and breathe."

But as Elton sorted out his life and courageously faced up to his personal problems, there were enough old recordings in the locker to fill the musical gap. As well as the previously mentioned 'Very Best Of' collection, the singer was also the subject of a US-released box set, 'To Be Continued…', which went as far back as the first single he'd written for Bluesology, plus some rarities and four new tracks. One of these was 'You Gotta Love Someone', which also made an appearance on the soundtrack of Tom Cruise's *Days Of Thunder*.

The year also saw the sad death of Ryan White, a hemophiliac teenager from Indianapolis who'd contracted the AIDS virus through a tainted transfusion. Elton, who'd become a friend of the family and was inspired by their dignity, sang his early song 'Skyline Pigeon' at his funeral, as well as being one of the boy's pallbearers. Believing the reissue success of 'Sacrifice' to have been something of a windfall, he pledged to give the royalties from that, and every subsequent single, to fight the killer disease. Perhaps as a reflection of the beastly way the 1980s had ended, the coming decade would see much more of the caring Elton John.

Left The astounding success of 'Sacrifice' on its reissue led to several awards, including this one from ASCAP in 1990. The royalties from his singles have since been dedicated to funding vital AIDS research.

Opposite Dressed like a genie from the *Arabian Nights*, Elton takes the concept of a turban several steps beyond the limit with this colorful creation.

Below The box set treatment has been accorded to many rock artists over the past decade as compact disks have become the industry standard. Few, however have been as handsomely packaged or as richly deserved as 'To Be Continued…', the US-originated collection of Elton John's best work, released in 1990.

1991 ★ 1996

Above Backstage with Madonna at the Brit Awards, 1991. Elton was awarded Best British Male Artist, but Madonna had to make do with her third nomination.

Previous page Soulful harmonies with Little Richard, whom Elton had backed while with Bluesology and would partner on his forthcoming album 'Duets'.

Opposite Elton shows the way as RuPaul shows a leg. The odd couple would co-present the 1994 Brits, an event more memorable for Take That's Beatles impersonation.

Below Sharing Elton's sense of fun, Tina Turner was delighted to add her own version of 'The Bitch Is Back' to the 'Two Rooms' album.

Having sloughed off much of his old life and possessions

like a snake shedding its skin, Elton John moved back into Woodside from a rented house in London's Holland Park—and promptly gained a 'gong' to decorate his comparatively bare mantelpiece. A Brit for Best British Male Artist was not a bad way to kick off 1991—and certainly the good grace with which it was collected was in stark comparison to the tantrum that had accompanied his acceptance in 1986. On that particular occasion, he'd expressed the opinion that the ceremony "makes good television—otherwise it's worthless." During this year's awards, Elton was pictured backstage in a posed embrace with Madonna, perhaps one of the few artists in the world who could empathize with the strains of fame he had borne for the past two decades.

The success of 'Sacrifice' was later reflected with the award of two Ivors—but this, unusually, would be a year in which Elton John released no album. Instead, his friends did it for him in the form of a tribute collection entitled 'Two Rooms' after the autobiographical '21 At 33' album track. Oleta Adams, Bon Jovi, Sinead O'Connor, and others would put their admiration for Elton into cover versions of his songs, ranging from the legendary to the little-known.

Each artist had his or her own reason for choosing their song. Clapton said 'Border Song' reminded him of "when I first met Elton—I could feel a way of doing it with a horn section in a bluesy kind of way." Sting had played 'Come Down In Time', a song the ex-Police man called "a strange story with evocative images," from 'Tumbleweed Connection' in the early days. It was interesting that there was more from the period between 'Your Song' and 'Rocket Man' on this album than on the 'Very Best Of', which had overlooked that creative but uncommercial era completely. Success and influence were clearly two different things. Kate Bush's reggae-tinged version of 'Rocket Man' was released as a single and, in reaching Number 12, came within ten chart places of the original.

Charitable Intentions

With no album of his own to promote, Elton could legitimately take a break from world touring, though this wouldn't stop him making a few choice appearances. Two in particular, both at Wembley, would bring smiles to the faces of a couple of friends. In March, he was backstage at a George Michael gig at Wembley Arena when they decided to duet on a song. Surprisingly, perhaps, their choice would not be 'Wrap Her Up', not 'Candle In The Wind' (on which they'd dueted at Wembley Stadium six years earlier) but 'Don't Let The Sun Go Down On Me'. Elton's surprise entry sent the crowd into raptures, and the performance—which was being taped, as Michael's concerts routinely were—would be issued in November to benefit the Terrence Higgins Trust AIDS charity.

Above Newly-weds 'Rachel' and Rod Stewart share a Wembley microphone. The pair's association dated back to the 1960s and was cemented by Rod's contribution of 'Your Song' to 'Two Rooms'.

Right Queen's Freddie Mercury gives Elton a Flash. The two, often camp, showmen had much in common, and John Reid had also managed this group in the 1970s. The singer's death hit his friend particularly hard.

Below The chart-topping team of Elton John and George Michael refuse to let the sun go down. Elton had been against releasing the pair's transatlantic hit, leaving a message on Michael's phone that he should "think twice."

A couple of weeks later, on April Fool's Day, Elton glammed himself up in a parody of Rod Stewart's new wife, New Zealand-born supermodel Rachel Hunter, and strutted on to the self-same Wembley stage to surprise his old pal and to duet, appropriately enough, on 'You're In My Heart'. If it was a surprise to Rod, it certainly wasn't to his other half, who allegedly helped out her 'double' in the make-up department!

Sad Goodbyes

As the year ended with the George Michael duet version of 'Don't Let The Sun…' at Number 1, its AIDS-fundraising function was all too sadly underlined. On 24 November, rock had said farewell to one of its master showmen, and Elton to a dear friend, when Freddie Mercury became the latest and most illustrious name to be added to the roll call of victims of the pernicious disease. He'd remained creative to the end, the fruits of his final recording sessions surfacing in 1995 as the 'Made In Heaven' album. Elton introduced a BBC-TV tribute the following night with the heartfelt statement: "Quite

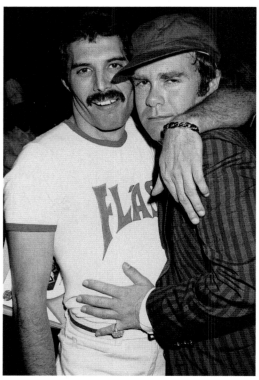

simply, he was one of the most important figures in rock'n'roll in the last 20 years"— words that could, of course, have applied equally to himself.

There was undoubtedly a feeling of "there but for the grace of God go I", and Elton, having ended 1990 with a confessional series of programs on Radio 1 entitled *Reg On The Radio*, indulged in another end-of-year report with David Frost. This time his soul-baring was for the benefit of American TV, and he gave Frost the full works on his problems with drink, drugs, and bulimia. His mother, he revealed, had moved to Spain to distance herself from her son's excesses, but had now returned to Britain, while he reflected on the fact that wife Renate, "a wonderful girl," had faced an impossible task living with him in his unreconstructed state. The pair were no longer in contact, at her request, but had not officially divorced.

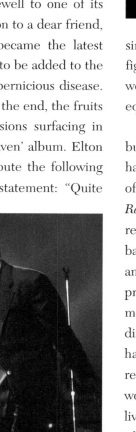

Elton introduced a tribute to Mercury with the heartfelt words: "Quite simply, he was one of the most important figures in rock'n'roll in the last 20 years"

Left As rock celebrated the life and work of Freddie Mercury, the partnership of Elton John and Guns N'Roses singer Axl Rose was one of the most unusual at Wembley Stadium. The occasion was an emotional one, and Elton was a notable absentee from the all-star finale.

Below Elton and Queen guitarist Brian May console each other at Freddie's funeral in November 1991. Early the following year, Elton would be mourning another friend— long-time bassist Dee Murray, who died in America of a stroke.

Below inset Elton's floral tribute—100 pink roses with a card reading "Thanks for being my friend: I will love you always." The sad loss of Mercury, both as a friend and a musician, added further impetus to Elton's personal crusade against AIDS, to which he would devote much of his time in the 1990s.

Having lost a friend in Freddie Mercury, Elton had to accept an equally bitter blow in January 1992, when Dee Murray gave up a long-running fight against cancer. Since his final appearance in the ranks of the Elton John Band he, like his former boss, had made his home in the States: March would see Elton pay his final respects to a man who'd held down the bass end on some of his greatest recordings by playing two benefit concerts for his widow, Maria, at Nashville's Grand Ole Opry.

Bohemian Rhapsody

The following month saw a rather larger stage resound to Elton's voice when, along with half of the hard-rock world, he took to the stage at Wembley Stadium to pay tribute to Freddie Mercury. His presence was no surprise—but dueting with Guns N'Roses singer Axl Rose most certainly was. The

American had made clear his distaste for homosexuals in a song, 'One in A Million', that had seen his group draw flak from the gay rights movement—but Elton put aside any antipathy, perhaps mindful of the fact that Rose had credited Mercury and his group with helping him through a deeply unhappy childhood and into a music career. It proved the start of an unlikely friendship.

The pair dueted on 'Bohemian Rhapsody', Queen's biggest hit and one that had topped the charts both in 1975 and on reissue as a tribute to its singer. It was a number so difficult to reproduce on stage that Queen themselves had resorted to using tapes and projections—but the day's most unlikely double act pulled it off. An emotionally drained Elton, however, was noticeably absent from the finale, but in September would guest on piano with the Gunners at the MTV *Music Awards* in Los Angeles.

Above Elton's relationship with partner David Furnish would prove a stabilizing influence in the 1990s. They are pictured here at Versace's 'Versus' show at Bryant Park, New York. Elton's 1992 tour, the first for three years, had stage and costumes designed by the Italian maestro.

Below On stage at Elizabeth Taylor's AIDS Benefit with George Michael, Whoopi Goldberg, Lionel Richie, and the hostess. This took place at Madison Square Garden on 11 October 1992 in front of a sellout audience.

Sharing the Spotlight

A series of double-header shows with Eric Clapton in 1992 would promote the release of 'The One', Elton's first album of new material for very nearly three years. If awards were still given for album sleeves in these days of miniaturized CD inserts, then this would clearly have qualified, having been conceived—as were the band's clothes and the stage decoration—by the Italian designer Gianni Versace.

Clapton shared the spotlight both vocally and instrumentally on 'Runaway Train', and Pink Floyd's Dave Gilmour contributed a trademark solo to 'Understanding Women', while the title track was a big ballad in classic Elton style that rightly became the first single. Yet it was 'The Last Song' that was singled out as being the keynote track, its themes of loss and deathbed reconciliation having a resonance not merely in Freddie Mercury's recent passing but also in Elton's unsatisfactory relationship with his father.

The sound was as elaborate as a layer cake, extra keyboards being added by Guy Babylon (a recent addition to the live band) and Mark Taylor, while the rhythm section consisted of ex-Eurythmics drummer Olle Romo and fretless bass wizard Pino Palladino, who'd been an integral part of Paul Young's sound in the previous decade. Critics could claim a triumph of style over substance, but the pent-up demand for new Elton recordings helped the album soar to Number 2 in the UK chart, just failing to unseat fellow keyboard-player Lionel Richie. America, too, gave it the thumbs-up, voting it a Number 8 success, while the single 'Simple Life' made history when it entered the charts, by giving Elton the greatest number of consecutive years (24) with a single in the Top 40— more than the great Elvis Presley!

The world tour that promoted 'The One' was punctuated by charitable appearances— for Neil Young's special school The Bridge and an Elizabeth Taylor AIDS benefit to name but two. In March 1993 he inaugurated the Elton John Aids Foundation with what would become an annual post-Oscar party in Beverly Hills. Having signed (with Bernie) a reported £26-million music publishing deal the previous November with Warner Chappell music that dated back to their 1974 compositions, Elton was clearly not short of cash—but he was to make fundraising for the Foundation a central pillar of his new, 'cleaned-up' life.

Harmony in South Africa

The year of 1993 was to involve the usual amount of globetrotting: in June the French Government honored him as an 'Officer of Arts and Letters', while the same month he proved he'd not totally lost his ability to lose his cool. Together with his entourage, he returned to London in reported high dudgeon when Tel Aviv airport failed to offer him the usual red carpet treatment and the Hilton was packed with pressmen. Eventually he relented and returned. He also revisited Sun City, scene of a contentious concert a decade earlier, but this time in harmonious circumstances to help celebrate South Africa's new regime.

Fans had to wait until the year's end to enjoy a new album but, after the wait for 'The One', 'Duets' was nothing less than prompt!

"Elton was to make fund-raising for the Foundation a central pillar of his new, 'cleaned-up' life"

Above A break in rehearsals for Aretha Franklin's 1993 TV special, in which he sang her 'Spirit In The Dark' and they dueted on 'Border Song'. Her decision to cover the latter title in the early 1970s added greatly to Elton's credibility as a singer-songwriter —a favor he was unlikely to forget.

Left Elton enjoys the freedom of the stage, having at least one other keyboard in the band to cover his absence from the ivories. It also enhanced his potential as a designer clothes horse, with Versace his favorite.

Right Elton holds up the designer spectacles that bear his name, the profits from their sales going to his AIDS Foundation. Those who share his charitable aims can now obtain an Elton John phone card, while the 'Elton' candle is just one of a wide range of other fund-raising concepts.

Center right Pictured at a New York City press conference on 5 September 1992, Elton pledges to donate the royalties from all his future American singles to combat AIDS. Two years earlier, he had made a similar statement concerning the royalties earnings from his UK singles.

Right The 1992 world tour was sponsored by cosmetics giants Revlon—hence this photo opportunity with supermodel Claudia Schiffer. Although Elton's stage presentations over the years have been as blatant as they have been stylish, his 1990s image was clearly the product of considerable thought and expense.

Right A charity mixed doubles match saw Elton and long-time friend Billie-Jean King (in spectacles) take on John McEnroe and Chris Evert. The death of former Wimbledon Champion Arthur Ashe from AIDS focused the sport's attention on the killer illness.

Left Early 1992 saw Elton unveiling his new hairstyle. Gone was the thinning thatch of yesteryear, to be replaced by luxuriant locks. The all-concealing hats of previous decades were consigned to the auction room as he ventured bare-headed into the future.

Below left Attending a Versace party in the company of Bob Geldof and Naomi Campbell. Elton and Geldof had both made a name as fund-raisers in addition to their pop-star personalities but, unlike the Live Aid supremo, Elton had not been overshadowed by his charity work.

Below Elton congratulates Steven Spielberg and Tom Hanks on their Oscars. In 1997, he would be working on a Spielberg project entitled *El Dorado*. This animated feature, scheduled to be screened in November 1999, told the story of two adventurers seeking their fortune in the mythical Spanish city.

Right Taupin, Barlow, and John—not the latest partnership of jet-set lawyers, but our favorite song-writing duo with the ex-Take That star. Elton took a keen interest in encouraging the younger generation of British pop penmen, and the Ivor-winning Barlow would contribute vocals to *The Lion King* project.

Below Back in court to refute another tabloid tale that turned out to be groundless. With so much of his private life having been revealed in legal actions, little remained for a scandal-hungry public to speculate over.

Below The program carried a clear statement of intent from piano men Elton John and Billy Joel as they teamed up on tour for the first of three occasions to date. In 1998 they were to bring their stage show to Britain for the first time, while a joint recording project remained a strong possibility.

Leonard Cohen, Little Richard, Stevie Wonder, Tammy Wynette, Kiki Dee, and kd lang (though no Rod Stewart) were among those with whom Mr John was prepared to share the spotlight and a microphone. Predictably, perhaps, it was the 1976 chart-topping pairing of Elton and Kiki who pulled out a Top 3 Christmas hit in 'True Love', the Grace Kelly/Bing Crosby vehicle from 1956's *High Society* movie. 'Duets' reached the UK Top 5, but struggled to make the *Billboard* Top 30.

Before he could say good-bye to a satisfactory year, Elton had to cross swords with Fleet Street once more when *The Mirror*, once his ally, printed an unsubstantiated article embellishing reports of his bulimia problem under the shameful headline 'Elton's Diet Of Death' (a £350,000 award to Elton was later cut to £75,000 on appeal). Just as sadly, he resigned as a director of Watford Football Club, having given way as chairman three years

earlier to millionaire car dealer Jack Petchey. He would, however, remain an ardent fan, and wherever in the world his travels took him he was frequently on the phone for results and news.

January 1994 brought another meeting with Axl Rose, who this time was not dueting with Elton but inducting him into the US Rock'n'Roll Hall of Fame. Fresh from that awards ceremony, the bespectacled one hosted the Brits in London on Valentine's Day with US drag artist RuPaul. The pair had collaborated before, on 'Duets', in an updated version of 'Don't Go Breaking My Heart', but the general feeling was that Elton could do better than this bizarre double act.

Talking of double acts, three more presented themselves in quick succession: Bob Geldof's ex-wife Paula Yates, who interviewed him on Channel 4 TV's *Big Breakfast*; Take That's Gary Barlow, to whom he'd present an Ivor in May in shades of George Michael; and Billy Joel, with whom he performed on a 21-date US sellout tour (the idea would be revived in 1995 and, for the first time in Britain, in 1998).

Getting Animated

The big news of the year was Elton's first soundtrack since *Friends* (which had itself reappeared on CD the previous year as part of a 37-track 'Rare Masters' package). Disney's animated *The Lion King* offered him the chance to rekindle a partnership with lyricist Tim Rice that had been briefly struck in the early 1980s 'Jump Up' era. And for Elton it was a chance to emulate *The Jungle Book*, his own favorite Disney animation, which had been released in 1967, the year he met Bernie.

His new lyric partner Rice had been first on to *The Lion King* project, and, when asked who he would like to work with, "said Elton, thinking they'd never get him. And to my utter amazement they did!" The project had taken the best part of two years, on and off, creating five songs (he'd later add three more when the film was turned into a stage musical in 1997). Incidental music was supplied by soundtrack specialist Hans Zimmer and was included on the album.

'Circle Of Life' and 'Can You See The Love Tonight', the two Top 20 singles, were the most impressive of the John-Rice contributions. Both could have claimed a place on any of his albums as ballads in the classic style and stood up as songs in their own right. 'I Just Can't Wait To Be King' and 'Hakuna Matata' were rather more stage musical in form, with echoes of Rice's previous work in the likes of *Joseph And The Technicolor Dreamcoat*. Even so, the latter—a set-piece for Timon the meerkat and Pumbaa the warthog to persuade the young lion Simba that he should adopt their 'worry-free' philosophy—had kids coming up and chanting the catchy mantra at Elton wherever he went!

Adding their backing vocals to the recording were Take That's Gary Barlow and Rick Astley, a former bill-topper at the Prince's Trust who'd since fallen on hard times. Was Elton, who'd backed Astley on a 1991 album, doing his Svengali bit again? Impossible to tell, but he'd certainly rediscovered his urge to socialize. George Michael and comedienne Dawn French had been among his guests at dinners that could number up to 30,

"The Lion King was a chance for Elton to emulate The Jungle Book, his own favorite Disney animation"

while a special November evening saw big-screen giants Richard Gere and Sylvester Stallone hob-nobbing with royalty in the shape of Princess Diana, a big fan of them both. Tim Rice, who'd turned 50 the previous day, was serenaded and given a cake.

Below Although he no longer spent most of each year on the road, Elton continued to grace the live music scene in the 1990s.

Right Relaunching Rocket Records with Ryan Downe and RuPaul. Other artists with whom the label aimed to revive itself in the late 1990s included Baltimore band Jimmie's Chicken Shack and New York singer-songwriter Daniel Cartier. English acts were being sought to complete the roster.

Center right Who's that girl? Tongue firmly in cheek, Elton camps it up with Australian soap star turned pop singer and gay icon Kylie Minogue for the pro-gay Stonewall '95 event. A thunderous reception at Stonewall proved his popularity with the gay community.

Bottom right Elton and Tim Rice show off their Academy Awards for Disney's *The Lion King*. The soundtrack sold over ten million copies worldwide, while the film would be converted into a hit Broadway show that opened in late 1997.

Right Elton bares his soul on stage. Among his concert appearances in the 1990s were two Moscow shows at the Kremlin Palace of Congress—16 years on from his first visit.

Left At New York's Waldorf Astoria Hotel, Elton is inducted into the Rock'n'Roll Hall of Fame, one of the few musical accolades that he hadn't received in the preceding quarter of a century. Elton was keen that Bernie, a vital component of his stateside success, should share in this honor.

Bottom left Another unlikely partner for Elton. This time the event is the 1995 Brits, and his consort is Lily Savage. Elton was to be presented by Sting with an Outstanding Contribution to the British Music Industry award and would perform his current single 'Believe'.

Below Once more unto the Brits, dear friend… Elton goes Brit-pop with Blur lead singer Damon Albarn, whose group picked up awards for Best Single, Best Video, Best Album (all for 'Parklife') and Best British Act.

Made In England

Musicians Elton John (piano, keyboards, harmonium, vocals), Davey Johnstone (guitar, mandolin, banjo, vocals), Bob Birch (bass, vocals), Ray Cooper (percussion), Charlie Morgan (drums), Guy Babylon (keyboards, programming, vocals), Paul Carrack (organ), Teddy Borowiecki (accordion), Paul Brennan (pipes, flute), Dermont Crehan (violin) • **Recorded at** Air Studios, Lyndhurst Hall, London • **Top 20 hit singles** 'Believe' (UK 15/US 13) • 'Made In England' (UK 18/US 52) • 'Please' (UK 33) • 'Blessed' (US 34) • **Unusual fact** Producer Greg Penny, best known for his work on kd lang's 'Ingenue' album, had first met Elton when a teenage fan at the 'Yellow Brick Road' sessions • **Track listing** Believe • Made In England • House • Cold • Pain • Belfast • Latitude • Please • Man • Lies • Blessed • **Commentary** Suddenly, Elton John was hip again—and the *New Musical Express*, the paper where the fateful ad for songwriters that brought EJ and BT together had appeared back in 1967, was happy to put him on the cover for the first time in living memory. Paul Buckmaster was back arranging, with George Martin doing likewise on just one track, the French Horn giving 'Latitude' a Beatles-y touch. This would be Elton's first release in the US for Island, MCA being allowed to issue a 'Love Songs' compilation instead. And Bernie absented himself from the States for the longest time he'd spent in Britain for 15 years to be around in the studio, topping Elton up with lyrics when needed. A three-year wait for a new Elton John album had, by common consent, been worth it • **Elsewhere in 1995...** Oasis top the UK singles chart for the first time with 'Some Might Say' • The Glastonbury Festival celebrates its 25th anniversary • Richey Edwards, guitarist with the Manic Street Preachers, disappears • Blur win the Brit-pop battle against Oasis • Kenny Everett, Viv Stanshall, Jerry Garcia, and Rory Gallagher die • REM drummer Bill Berry suffers brain hemorrhage during Swiss gig • TV's *Soldier Soldier* stars Robson and Jerome score two UK Number 1s • George Michael signs to new label after a court battle with Sony • The surviving Beatles release 'Free As A Bird', complete with John Lennon vocals

Released March 1995

Chart Position UK 3

Chart Position US 13

Producer Greg Penny and Elton John

Tim and Elton's work on *The Lion King* had resulted in two Grammy awards and also gathered an Oscar for Best Song—a trophy that would be given pride of place among the gold record sales awards at Woodside and which he accepted in the name of his grandmother, Ivy Sewell, who had died the week before and who, he said, had first sat him down at the piano at age three.

Outstanding Achievement

The fortunes of Rocket Records, for so long a 'custom' label for Elton despite a bright and more varied start, were due to improve too. It was relaunched in January 1995 with singer-songwriter Ryan Downe. But the main event of the year was the March release of 'Made In England', an album that backed Elton's assertion, when presented with an Outstanding Achievement in Music Brit just weeks earlier, that "there's life in the old girl yet!"

The new name in the producer's chair (sharing responsibility with Elton) was Greg Penny, who'd clearly made an impression when he supervised kd lang's contribution to the 'Duets' album. The record had been kept under wraps for the best part of a year to avoid interfering with his film career, and the first single, 'Believe', was set upon with gusto by Elton-starved radio stations. Its own Number 4 chart placing was recognition that this was an album of old-style favorites, with plenty of single word titles, such as 'Please', 'Man', 'Lies', and 'Pain'.

'Believe', a Number 15 single, was the first song Elton wrote for the album that he'd been happy with, discarding the first few as was his custom. Little wonder its optimistic vibe put it at the very start of proceedings, as well as making it the first single. He was happy that 'Belfast' (a song about the troubled Northern Ireland city, featuring pipes, flutes, and accordion) saw "the good in the situation as opposed to just the bad," a terrorist ceasefire having been established in the time that elapsed between recording and release. The title song both satirized and celebrated the attitudes of the mother country, but also came across as a kind of trademark of quality.

The album's gold success saw six early albums reissued in May, remastered and with extra tracks: 'Yellow Brick Road' was condensed on to a single CD, though those with long memories and the original triple gatefold would sigh at the miniaturized packaging.

New Year's Honors

May brought two more awards: the King of Sweden presented him with the Polar Music Prize, while later in the month came another Ivor, this time for 'Circle Of Life'. Two concerts at Moscow's Palace of Congress were the year's major gigs as Elton toured the new album, pausing in November to undertake some fundraising at New York's Hard Rock Café for AIDS research. His good works saw him win recognition in the 1996 New Year's Honours list with the award of Commander of the British Empire—those in the know suggested it would have been sooner but for the tabloid muckraking.

In June, Elton linked up with Luciano Pavarotti (of 'Nessun Dorma' fame) for a live performance in aid of the War Child charity, giving his public persona yet another shine, but a 'fly-on-the-wall' style TV documentary made by long-time partner David Furnish

and entitled *Tantrums And Tiaras* showed him in a much less flattering light. As ever, though, it was the public Elton everybody really wanted, and, aside from the tabloids, few were paying much attention to his private life. There were now a couple of top-notch Elton imitators, Elton Jack from Australia and Elton Oliver from England. Should he lose the inclination to tour and decide to announce another 'retirement', it was suggested, he could always send one of them out in his stead!

Above Elton and Pavarotti join forces for War Child, in June 1996. The heavyweight duo recorded their double act with 'Live Like Horses' later that same year. Elton also supported a charity performance of Mozart's 'Magic Flute'.

Opposite Mellow in yellow. General opinion held that 'Made In England' was Elton's most rounded album since 'Sleeping With The Past' and, with its 1970s reference points, it harked back to his halcyon days.

Left Fundraising for charity at New York's Hard Rock Café in November 1995 as World AIDS Day approaches, Elton displays his 'personalized' T-shirt.

Above Keeping mum on his 50th birthday, celebrated by a giant costume party at London's Hammersmith Palais and attended by hundreds of celebrity friends. Dance music was provided by DJ for the night Boy George, while a flag with Elton's crest and motto flew overhead.

Previous page The first of two funerals for a friend. Elton looks on as murdered fashion designer Gianni Versace is buried. "The world has lost a wonderful creative genius and I have lost a very dear friend," said Elton, who had been on holiday in the south of France when he heard the news.

Opposite In full regalia as the birthday party gets in to full swing. His three-foot high powdered wig was topped off with a model galleon that blew smoke out of its cannons.

If Her Majesty the Queen hadn't coined the term

Annus Horribilis, then it's doubtful Elton John would have. After all, Latin wasn't one of his specialist subjects at Pinner Grammar—but the sentiment was one he'd come to know only too well as 1997 unfolded. The year appeared to start so well. Settled in a permanent relationship with Canadian advertising executive turned film-maker David Furnish, with a new album on the stocks and a movie in the pipeline, he was set to celebrate his half-century in style.

But just as his 40th had been marred by that infamous run-in with *The Sun*, so, ten years on, fate was to decree that while Elton's 50th birthday was indeed an event to be savored, two bolts from the blue later in the year would rob him of firm friends and cause him to muse on his own mortality.

The omens had been good when he sailed into the year on the UK Top 10 singles success of 'Live Like Horses', a song he'd performed with a very special duet partner, Luciano Pavarotti. The Italian tenor had, like Elton, busied himself with good works, most notably the War Child charity, which had seen him join forces with U2 on a memorable rendition of 'Miss Sarajevo'. Now it was Elton's turn—and the song chosen was 'Live Like Horses', in which Pavarotti sang his responses in Italian. Bernie would reveal, though, that the song had not been written expressly for the purpose: "that was Elton's idea." As for having him sing in his native tongue, "have you ever heard an Italian try to say 'horses'?" Elton would revisit the song solo on the new album.

As mentioned, Elton's golden jubilee was fast approaching—and an invitation to the party was society's hot ticket as 6 April approached. Hammersmith Palais, itself a reasonably-sized central London rock venue, was hired for the evening—and though it shut its doors for good later in the year, that was no reflection on the behavior of Elton's revelers. All had to arrive in fancy dress, and Elton—with a purple-wigged David Furnish by his side—was obviously going to be no exception. More than that, his robes were so extravagant he had to be transported to the feast in the back of a fair-sized lorry!

Sweetly Scented

The party organizers had been working at the Palais since the previous night's revelers had finally been ejected at four in the morning. It would take 12 hours' work by a dozen-strong cleaning team to eradicate the lingering smell of beer and cigarettes, an operation finally completed by the lighting of scented candles. A high-class florist supplied 15-foot pillars entwined with delphinium, lilies, and roses, while pink, blue, and green lights illuminated tables covered with leopard-print cloths. Nine Asian and eight Italian dishes were on the menu—little wonder six months' planning had gone into the event!

The guests ranged widely, from musicians Phil Collins and Brian May to Lord Lloyd Webber, who lowered the tone somewhat by wearing Leyton Orient football kit! As well as the elaborate official birthday cake, Elton was presented at the door with a piano-shaped alternative from the pop columnist at the tabloid he'd once battled long and hard with. "Have a Bizarre birthday from all at *The Sun*", read the inscription—no wonder he was tight-lipped as the obligatory picture was taken!

Another anniversary being celebrated alongside his half-century was 30 years in harness with the faithful Taupin. "We're like brothers," said Elton, claiming they never had a major argument and it was the fact they both pursued outside projects that meant their relationship had survived intact. Bernie's lyrics had become "more musical" in recent years, having been supplied "by the yard" in the earliest days for Elton to nip and tuck as appropriate. Just to prove he was a musician as well as a writer of words, he'd formed a band in the States: 1997 was scheduled to see their second album from Farm Dogs (named, one suspects, in shades of the Brown Dirt Cowboy).

Musical Tastes

When still Reg Dwight, Captain Fantastic had haunted Musicland record shop in London's Soho listening to everything he could—and both an eclectic appetite and a hunger for music still raged within him. He'd reveal that he thought Oasis's Noel Gallagher wrote "brilliant songs—and that's the key to everything," but reserved his highest praise for three-piece Dodgy, claiming "they remind me of the Who." He also enjoyed watching Blur at the Brits, but although his tastes even extended to dance acts like the Chemical Brothers, Prodigy, and the Underworld, he realized there was nothing he could readily incorporate into his own music. "It's the sound that will take us into the next millennium," he declared, adding that he found "that kind of music incredibly exciting." In the next breath, though, he cited 'Prisoner Of Love' as what happens when Elton John follows trends.

The success of *The Lion King* (which had followed up its box-office success by selling 26 million video copies in its first fortnight) had helped Elton reach a new generation of potential fans, even though he could still joke about it. "I was sitting there at the piano thinking 'I'm writing a song about a f**king warthog, this is the end of my career!'" Recognizing the benefit, he collaborated again with Tim (now Sir Tim) Rice, and turned the handful of original songs

Below The tabloid that had proved the bane of Elton's life in the 1980s aims to kiss and make up with its own birthday cake. Elton seems less than amused behind the painted smile.

HAVE A BIZARRE BIRTHDAY ELTON FROM ALL AT THE Sun

they'd contributed to the film into what was effectively a new musical. After playing round the States in the autumn of 1997, it opened on Broadway in mid-November.

The pair had been commissioned to pursue another exciting, but very different, project—a 25-song musical of Guiseppe Verdi's *Aida*. The prospect of following Joe Green, as Elton cheekily dubbed the late Italian opera maestro, didn't seem to daunt him one bit. Also on the cards was *El Dorado*, a full-length animation for Steven Spielberg's Dreamworks organization.

The new album was to be toured in the States in October, playing more intimate venues than previously, before hitting home soil with a band for the first time in some years. After that was a reunion with Billy Joel. They'd had so much fun playing the States in 1994 and 1995, Elton

explained, that he'd told his piano-man buddy "We should take this around the world before we're too old." The tour kicked off in the States in January, taking in Australia, Japan and the Far East before British stadium shows scheduled for June 1998 at Rangers' Ibrox football ground in Glasgow, Lancashire Cricket Club's Old Trafford headquarters and two at his time-honored favorite, Wembley Stadium, a stone's throw from Pinner. There was little doubt the local hero would sell out like all his previous solo appearances there.

Above Elton saw nothing wrong with growing old, "as long as you maintain an interest" in new music—and alternative chart-toppers The Prodigy were among the 1990s groups for whom he expressed admiration.

Left inset The lorry in which the ever-genial host was transported to his half-century celebration was fitted out with gilt-framed pictures, burgundy velvet drapes, and thrones for Elton and his friend David Furnish.

After the fun they had had on their earlier States tour, he told Billy Joel "We should take this around the world before we're too old."

Right Rehearsing to save the rain forest with an all-star cast including Billy Joel, Paul Simon, and Sting. Elton first backed the cause in 1991 at the second annual Rainforest Foundation benefit show at Carnegie Hall, New York, singing 'Come Down In Time' with Sting, and appeared again in 1994.

Right At the Empire film awards with the Monty Python team of Michael Palin, Terry Jones, and Terry Gilliam. Elton was always a fan of humor, and in 1981 had paid £14,000 for original scripts from radio's Goon Show

Below right Showing off sales records for *The Lion King*. The soundtrack album spawned two hit singles in 'Can You Feel The Love Tonight' and 'Circle Of Life', the former picking up an Oscar for Best Original Song. It would also win an award for Most Played Song on US radio and television.

Left Although 1997 was the year for the Spice Girls, Eleton was still around to help hand out the awards. Fellow 1970s survivors The Bee Gees kept him company in a Brits Awards ceremony that celebrated Girl Power at London's Earl's Court in February.

Below left An employee of Bonhams auction house models yet another item of Elton-abilia to go under the hammer, in September 1997. As well as disposing of memorabilia in this way, Elton also held an AIDS charity shop sale during 1997, under the banner 'Out of the Closet'.

Below With Donatella and Gianni Versace before the design guru's untimely death in Miami. Elton, Sting, Jon Bon Jovi, and other top rock stars were to join the fashion world to honour his memory with a celebration of his life in December 1997.

Right The effect of Versace's death on the fashion world was compared by critics to that of John Lennon, another of Elton's friends whose creative spirit was violently extinguished at its peak.

Opposite The Rocket Man and the People's Princess. Having met Diana back in the early 1980s at Prince Andrew's 21st birthday party, Elton had suffered with her as the Royal romance withered and died.

Below Seated next to Diana, Elton is comforted by David Furnish at Versace's funeral on 22 July 1997. "We were so close," said Elton, "that it is like a large part of my life has died with him."

That was the schedule—but, as Elton had discovered, the best-laid plans can go awry. They certainly hadn't included waking up to the news in July 1997 that Gianni Versace had been brutally slain outside his Miami mansion. The Italian designer had been a great friend: more than that, he'd designed and decorated the 1992 album 'The One', and Elton had not only been a very public wearer of his creations but had also attended many of his fashion shows. Indeed, a January 1997 issue of the *Sunday Times Magazine* had depicted Elton as Versace's new supermodel.

At the funeral, a clearly distraught Elton was comforted by Princess Diana—little realizing, any more than the watching world, that just six weeks later she would be mourned on a global scale. Elton and the Princess had been friends, but there had apparently been a disagreement over a charity commitment and letters had been exchanged they'd both later regret.

A Candle Burns Out

Diana's death in a Paris underpass in the limousine she shared with boyfriend Dodi Fayed would still be the subject of speculation months later. But Elton was in no doubt that some musical response was the best contribution he could make to giving the nation a positive focus of grief. He immediately turned to his faithful wordsmith, and the call was answered within the hour by faxed new lyrics. But for which song?

Elton had, of course, written 'Song For Guy' in response to an early death, but had dealt with the lyric problem by not writing any. Similarly, 'Funeral For A Friend' was another atmospheric instrumental. Diana herself had loved 'Your Song', but though hers could well have been "the sweetest eyes" he'd ever seen, other lyrics about building "a big house where we both could live" were clearly unsuitable. 'Don't Let The Sun Go Down On Me' was a possibility, but it took so long to get to the chorus. The clear favorite was 'Candle In The Wind'—in his own words "the only song I've ever written where I get goose bumps every time I play it."

The song was eerily appropriate—a glamorous public figure and icon cut down in her prime, the victim of a prurient, intrusive press in life and endless speculation and innuendo in death. Yes, this was the right song—but again, the words...Diana had identified with the

Above With David Furnish at Diana's funeral in Westminster Abbey on 6 September 1997. Elton, who called Diana "a beautiful person and dear friend," later admitted he would willingly give up his fame and fortune to have her and Versace back again.

Below right Having been invited by the Royal family to perform, Elton put the thoughts of a nation into song with the help of his faithful lyricist Taupin. "His brilliance has never shone brighter," said Elton, referring to the new words.

Inset Sales of 'Candle In The Wind '97', produced by George Martin, broke all records and gave the song its third lease of life. The proceeds went to the charities Diana had worked with so closely.

original lyric, notably the lines about never knowing who to cling to, "they made you change your name", and the now all-too-apposite observation about being hounded by the press that would be echoed in Earl Spencer's speech.

There would be those who disapproved of such a tribute—Rolling Stone Keith Richards acidly remarked that Elton was making a habit of writing songs about "dead blondes"—but the announcement that he would be performing the song at the funeral was considered to represent her love of contemporary pop just as charity workers in the congregation would fly the flag for her selfless work for others.

The new lyrics Bernie faxed were, in some ways, easy to pick holes in—from the very first line. 'Goodbye England's Rose' was geographically accurate in reflecting her birthplace but ran the risk of alienating those, notably the Welsh, who'd adopted the Princess as their own: an easy mistake for someone long domiciled on foreign shores. Then there was the line

about "footsteps on England's greenest hills"— possibly inappropriate for someone clearly happiest in the city. But there was an echo of William Blake's 'Jerusalem' in the lyric that transcended such petty nitpicking.

The funeral service in Westminster Abbey was a harrowing experience for all concerned. Elton had elected to use an autocue, his biggest fear being that he'd slip back into the familiar lyric he'd sung every show for some two dozen years. In the event, he had no such problems and, with the eyes of the world upon him (31.5 million tuned in, ten million more than Diana's 1981 wedding), did a flawless job.

His first task after leaving the Abbey was to perform the song again for what he claimed would be the very last time. It would also be the last production of Sir George Martin, the Beatles' legendary producer, who was shortly set to retire at 71. No great arrangement or orchestra was needed, woodwind and a string quartet sufficing to subtly enhance the piano and vocal performance. The end result, committed to tape at London's Townhouse Studio, was not unlike another great Martin production, 'Yesterday', and Elton obliged by nailing the vocal on the second take.

Popular Approval

A standing ovation when Watford FC played local rivals Wycombe the next day (all Saturday sport having been postponed as a mark of respect) showed exactly how high Elton John stood in public regard. It certainly made a marked contrast to the chants of "Elton John's A Homosexual" he'd once had to endure. By the time Watford played their next match at 3.00pm the following Saturday, 1.5 million copies of the new recording would have passed across record-shop counters nationwide.

A special shift of over 1,000 workers had come in at a Blackburn pressing plant to make the release possible, but even so, could supply hope to keep up with demand? The UK singles sales record had been set in 1984 by Band Aid's 'Do They Know It's Christmas', at 3.5 million. 'Candle 97' had hit 3.2 million by the end of the first fortnight—and this, remember, was Britain alone. The next yardstick was Bing Crosby's 'White Christmas', rated by the *Guinness Book Of Records* as having sold 150 million copies worldwide (a figure which must include sales of every compilation on which it's ever appeared). In the States, 'Candle 97' racked up over five million after its third week atop the chart, with a further six million shipped and expected to be sold.

Back in 1973, Bernie Taupin had stated in *Rolling Stone* magazine that 'Candle' was "the best song we've ever written—it may come across as another schmaltzy song, but people can listen to it and realize what the writers feel for her." Certainly, it eclipsed 'competition' in the shape of Chris De Burgh's 'So Beautiful' (Number 29) and friend George Michael's 'You Have Been Loved' (Number 2), a coincidentally suitable release written originally by Michael to mourn a close friend and given added poignancy by the recent death of his mother.

Far from an Anticlimax

After all the drama that had preceded it, the late-September release of 'The Big Picture' could have been anticlimactic— especially since it did not contain the chart-topping song. But the British public clearly saw Elton as a relevant player in a chart dominated by Radiohead, Texas, and Ocean Colour Scene. Musically, guest appearances by the East London Gospel and Angel Voice choirs, plus guest organist Paul Carrack, added to the black music feel reminiscent of the (also Chris Thomas-produced) 'Sleeping With The Past'.

Above left Elton, along with George Michael (center) and many other representatives of the pop music world, were present to pay tribute to the one member of the Royal Family who seemed to be in touch with current trends.

Above Acknowledging the cheers of the crowd at Vicarage Road, Watford, the day after the funeral. A minute's silence was observed at this and other sporting occasions in the days following the sad event.

The Big Picture

Musicians Elton John (piano, organ, vocals), Davey Johnstone (guitar), John Jorgenson (guitar), Bob Birch (bass), Guy Babylon (keyboards), Paul Carrack (organ), Charlie Morgan (drums, percussion), Matthew Vaughan (keyboards, percussion), Paul Clarvis (tabla), Carol Kenyon (backing vocals), Jackie Rawe (backing vocals), East London Gospel Choir, Angel Voices Choir • **Recorded at** Townhouse Studios, London • **Top 20 hit singles** 'Something About The Way You Look Tonight'/'Candle In The Wind '97' (UK 1/US 1) • **Unusual fact** 'The Big Picture' completed a sequence of seven albums in the decade (beginning with 'Sleeping With The Past', which topped the chart in 1990, and including two compilations) that all reached the UK Top 5 • **Track listing** Long Way From Happiness • Live Like Horses • The End Will Come • If The River Can Bend • Love's Got A Lot To Answer For • Something About The Way You Look Tonight • The Big Picture • Recover Your Soul • January • I Can't Steer My Heart Clear Of You • Wicked Dreams • **Commentary** Two mirrors covered up in the artwork could refer to the death of Gianni Versace, to whom the album was dedicated: by the time of release, Elton was mourning another friend, although 'Candle '97' was sensibly not included on this disk. Nor would it really have fitted, because these were not observations, but songs about relationships. The packaging looked immediate, like a magazine—a running head on each page dates the release as 'Sept 97', while lyrics are pulled out like headlines. This was Elton (and Bernie) at their most immediate • Other magazines, however, didn't necessarily concur. Q, the style bible to which he'd given a candid interview back in 1995, gave it just two stars in a scant two-inch review, while the Rolling Stones' new effort received one more star and three-quarters of a page: clearly the excessive hipness quotient of 1995 had now settled back to more modest proportions • **Elsewhere in 1997...** Katrina and the Waves win the Eurovision Song Contest for UK • Oasis score the biggest album of the year in 'Be Here Now' • The Spice Girls bubble subsides as they sack their manager and second-album sales disappoint • US country-pop singer John Denver goes down with his plane in October • Parlophone release 'The Very Best Of John Lennon' • Bristol drum and bass act Roni Size and his group Reprazent win the Mercury Music Prize

Released October 1997

Chart Position UK 3

Chart Position US 9

Producer Chris Thomas

All the songs, he explained, with the exception of 'Live Like Horses', were "about relationships—either about good relationships or how difficult it is to have relationships or relationships that have gone bad." He could, he affirmed, relate to all three cases. All were very melodic, and he was justifiably proud of the result. The basic band had been augmented by a new member, American guitarist John Jorgenson who'd come to fame as a member of ex-Byrd Chris Hillman's Desert Rose Band before leading country-rock instrumentalists the Hellecasters whom he put on hold to join up with Elton. He'd play in tandem with old faithful Davey Johnstone, who in 1997 celebrated 25 years by Elton's side—still with the same 'rock-star' hairstyle!

Songs of Love

'Something About The Way You Look Tonight' had Top 10 written all over it even before it was paired with 'Candle In The Wind '97'—a rolling, flowing hymn of devotion destined to rank with Clapton's 'Wonderful Tonight' as a celebration of beauty. Taupin revealed that it had been his suggestion to write an album of songs that were "like standards", citing Sinatra and Tony Bennett as the litmus test for inclusion. And since most standards are romantically centered, the album became one of love songs—something that both men, in settled, simultaneous relationships, could empathize with.

Even song titles like 'Long Way From Happiness' and 'The End Will Come' disguised a surprisingly chirpy album. And when asked by *Billboard* magazine which song he was most looking forward to playing live, Elton nominated 'The River Can Bend', a song that explained

"In third world countries, some European countries, and in South America the AIDs situation is very grave indeed—so we have to carry on."

"never give up, there's always hope." The end result, clothed in a striking Elton portrait by Julian Schnabel, was dedicated "to the loving memory of Gianni Versace".

All in all, the record's success—it reached Number 9 in the States—looked set to add more millions to Elton's personal treasure chest. In September, the month before release, it had been revealed that he'd paid himself a cool £35.5 million the previous year, which represented a 300 per cent rise over 1995. He'd done this through the two companies, Happenstance and J Bondi, of whom he was the only employee.

There'd been a series of British TV shows offering viewers *An Audience With*— various showbiz icons, who deftly fielded prepared questions pitched (but gently) by a gathering of fellow celebs. As ever, Elton felt the show had to go on—indeed, had stated "you have to grieve and you have to move on"—and pitched up at the appointed time to carry off a bravura performance. *An Audience With Elton John* wasn't a television milestone, but it gave him the chance to wrest the spotlight away from past events and towards his new album. Not before, though, he'd given current pop idols the Spice Girls the chance to be Kiki Dee for a day and back him on the most woeful version of 'Don't Go Breaking My Heart' ever heard. Come back RuPaul, all was forgiven... November would see him give a more intimate audience to Oprah.

Despite the year of tragedies, the ongoing battle with AIDS was very much on his list of priorities. "It's something I'll probably be doing for the rest of my life now," he disclosed to *Music And Media* magazine

Left Elton coming out of the Montserrat fundraising event held at the Royal Albert Hall on 15 September 1997. The 4,500 tickets for the event, attended by the Duke of York, sold out within minutes and, together with the TV rights, raised over £500,000.

Opposite On tour, promoting 'The Big Picture' in the US. His return to Britain to play pre-Christmas 1997 dates revived an old tradition.

while patiently explaining that, though AIDS was beginning to find its level in North America and much of Europe, "in third world countries, some European countries, and in South America the situation is very grave indeed—so we have to carry on."

Another good cause to receive his attention was the Caribbean island where he'd recorded a successful trio of albums in the early 1980s. Montserrat was suffering from the eruption of a volcano, and George Martin, whose island studio spawned 'Too Low For Zero' among many other great albums had set up a charity concert, held at London's Royal Albert Hall on 15 September. Entitled 'Music For Montserrat', its aim to raise £750,000 was assisted by a 'pay-per-view' arrangement with Sky TV, and Mark Knopfler, Eric Clapton, and Sir Paul McCartney were among the acts happy to oblige.

"The time had now come, it seemed, for Elton to tell his own story his own way."

Above: Reunited with Graham Taylor, the man who led Watford during their glory days of the 1970s and early 1980s before moving on to Aston Villa and, eventually, England. The revival of the club's fortunes in 1997-98 was due to the renewed link between chairman and manager.

Opposite Stateside fans enjoy 'The Big Picture' tour from a front-row perspective. Elton appeared determined to end his Annus Horribilis—1997—on a high.

But charity, they say, begins at home—and Elton, having resumed his post as chairman of Watford at the start of the season, had promptly reinstated Graham Taylor in the team manager's job. As he took the Albert Hall stage, the Hornets were buzzing happily at the top of the Second (old Third) Division table. And the new striker intent on shooting them to a higher plane, was Ronnie 'Rocket' Rosenthal, an Israeli acquired on a free transfer from Tottenham whose appetite for goals must have delighted the original Rocket Man as much as his nickname!

Into the Future

The events of the past year had revived the idea of an Elton autobiography. He had granted co-operation to Philip Norman, author of the acclaimed Beatles biography *Shout!*, and the result had been the previously-mentioned *Elton*, first published in 1991 and updated a year later. This had until now been regarded as the nearest thing to an authorized story, since, "though denied direct access (Norman) received help from many of his closest friends, associates and members of his family." The time had now come, it seemed, for Elton to tell his own story his own way—and the project was touted at October's Frankfurt Book fair with a rumored £8 million price tag.

He wouldn't be doing the storytelling alone, American *Interview* magazine journalist Ingrid Sischy having been enlisted to lend her professional hand to Elton's pen. This, to some, negated the appeal of a 'warts and all' biography, especially since it remained to be seen what could be said that hadn't already been said publicly, privately, and in court. Meanwhile, Elton was warming up by giving his opinion of Keith Richards—who, it may be recalled, was uncomplimentary about the Diana tribute—to *Mojo* magazine. "They should have thrown Keith out of the Stones 10, 15 years ago—he's held them back. Mick's very forward-looking, and Keith's still listening to Otis Redding!" If this was a sample of the forthcoming book, the fur could be set to fly.

So the Elton John story looked set to roll on into a new millennium, whoever told it—and if, to misquote the lyric to 'I'm Still Standing', he was somewhat long in the tooth to feel like a little kid, he was undoubtedly entitled to consider himself a true survivor. With his work for the AIDS Foundation, he was helping others do the same. And his music continued to inspire millions, in good times and in bad. Although the 1998 New Year's Honours granted him a knighthood, it was unlikely to change the man who had touched the hearts of so many people.

Picture credits

Quadrillion Publishing Ltd would also like to thank the following:

Jeremy Thomas for the location and memorabilia photography (16t, 17b, 17t, 19tr, 22, 29b, 41t, 46b, 46t, 71tr, 79tr, 104bl, 104tl, 107br, 118b, 123cr.)

Brendan, Marion, Tom, and Jessie Glover for their help.

Alan at Wrap It Up, PO Box 220, Lincoln, England LN1 2RZ for his advice.